Laying

Community

foundations

for Your Child
with a Disability

How to Establish Relationships
That Will Support Your Child
after You're Gone

Linda J. Stengle, M.H.S.

All rights reserved under International and Pan-American copyright conventions. Published in the United States of America by Woodbine House, Inc., 6510 Bells Mill Rd., Bethesda, MD 20817. 800-843-7323.

The following individuals and organizations have graciously given permission to use extended quotations from their works: Wolf Wolfensberger, *Common Assets of Mentally Retarded People That Are Commonly Not Acknowledged* (pp. 43-45); David B. Schwartz, *Crossing the River* (pp. 7-9); Joan Gipple and Linda Anthony, The Pennsylvania Coalition of Citizens with Disabilities, *In Praise of Parents* (pp. 179-83); Emilee Curtis, New Hats, *Using Natural Supports in Community Integration* (pp. 56-59, 103-7).

Cover Illustration by: Becky Heavner
Cover/Book Design by: Brenda Ruby

Library of Congress Cataloging-in-Publication Data

Stengle, Linda J.
   Laying community foundations for your child with a disability : how to establish relationships that will support your child after you're gone / by Linda J. Stengle.
      p. cm.
   Includes bibliographical references and index.
   ISBN 0-933149-67-0 (pbk.)
   1. Handicapped--United States--Popular works. 2. Handicapped--United States--Family Relationships--Popular works. 3. Parents of handicapped children--United States--Popular works. 4. Social integration--United States--Popular works. 5. Estate planning--United States--Popular works. I. Title.
HV1553.S74 1996   96-18172
362.4'04083--dc20   CIP

Manufactured in the United States of America

10 9 8 7 6 5 4 3 2 1

With appreciation
to my husband, Paul,
who gave me the idea
for this book.

TABLE OF CONTENTS

Introduction vii

Chapter **1**
What Am I Going to Do? 1

Chapter **2**
What Can I Count on? 17

Chapter **3**
First Things First 29

Chapter **4**
How Do I Help Develop Relationships for My Child? ... 41

Chapter **5**
What about the Younger Child with Disabilities? 69

Chapter **6**
What about Brothers and Sisters? 85

Chapter **7**
How Do I Make Things Happen? 95

Chapter 8
How Have Others Incorporated These Ideas? 123

Chapter 9
How Do I Ask Someone to Make a Long-Term
Commitment to My Child? 133

Chapter 10
What Have Other People Done in My Situation? 145

Chapter 11
When Should I Make Some of These Changes? 167

Chapter 12
What If I Can't Get the Support I Need? 177

Appendix A
Publications about Wills, Estates, and Trusts 191

Appendix B
Resources for Planning for the Future 193

Appendix C
Resources for Advocacy 195

Appendix D
Indications of Abuse 199

Bibliography 205

Index 209

INTRODUCTION

During a program planning meeting near Philadelphia, a woman in her eighties listened carefully to the ideas the staff had for improving her son's performance at the workshop. When they had finished, they asked if she had anything she wanted to add. She said, "Can anyone help me with what's going to happen to Richie when I die? Is he going to have to go live in a state institution?"

The group was quiet, and it was clear that no one knew how to answer her question. Finally, the case manager said that there was no money for group home placements and that people whose parents had died would probably have to be placed in a state program.

The woman left with tears in her eyes.

The problem of long-term care plagues all parents of people with cognitive disabilities. People with cognitive disabilities are so vulnerable. Studies have found that abuse is rampant in institutions, and many people have concerns about the care in group homes as well. Plus, the whole field of developmental disabilities is in a state of change; many professionals agree that the current residential service system is crumbling.

There has been a lot written on the subject of future planning, but unfortunately most of it involves the management of inheritances through wills and trusts. Many parents fall into the trap of thinking that if their child has money, he'll be okay. But consider these two situations:

> *Joe's father left him $2 million in a trust fund designed to pay for his care. An arrangement was made with a private institution to house Joe for the rest of his life. While his future is secure, Joe is very unhappy. He used to talk and smile a lot; now he's withdrawn. His days are all pretty much the same: get up, eat breakfast with about twenty other people, go to workshop, come back to the cottage, watch TV, eat dinner, watch more TV, go to bed. Once every two weeks a recreation aide comes to the cottage to take four guys out to the mall for ice cream. Sometimes Joe gets to go, and sometimes he doesn't. He has been physically attacked by other people living with him, and once he was burned with a cigarette by a staff member who "didn't like his attitude." When someone visits Joe, he says, "Can I come live with you? I don't like it here."*

❖

> *William's mother died suddenly and was unable to leave behind any money for William's care. What she did provide him with was a rich and full church life. William and his mother attended church every Sunday and went to all church events. Members of the church knew and liked William. When his mother died, the reverend found out that the government was planning to send William to a state facility two hours away. He told the women in the congregation, who decided that they wanted William to live nearby and continue coming to church. A delegation from the church met with city officials and asked to work out an alternative living arrangement for William. The city officials agreed. Now, Richard lives in the same apartment building as one of the women from*

the church. She's teaching him how to cook and checks on him every day to see if he needs anything. He still attends church every Sunday and has started going to one of their Bible study groups. A social worker visits William regularly and there is talk of finding him a real job. When asked about how he spends his time, William says, "Mrs. Bellini's teaching me how to cook; she thinks I eat too much spaghetti." He says he misses his mom, but talks animatedly about his friends and church life. When asked about what's missing in his life, William says, "I want to get a girlfriend."

These two lives are markedly different. Joe's father had a lot of financial resources, but in his effort to provide his son with a permanent living situation, he locked Joe into an unhappy lifestyle. Since Joe lives far away in an institution, he has very little access to nondisabled friends or family. His relatives assume that the institution is taking care of all his needs, so they very rarely visit him or even think about him.

William's life, though less secure financially, seems rich and full. He has friends who care about him and things to look forward to, like getting a new job. If someone tried to take advantage of William, chances are one of his friends from church would step in and protect his interests. Though his life is not perfect, he knows he is loved and that he has a place in the heart of his friends.

Obviously, if you have the financial resources, money can help make your child's life more secure after you die. However, it is all too easy to have those funds drained by the government to reimburse the cost of maintaining your child in a group home, or, as we saw in Joe's case, to attach the money to a lifestyle that doesn't meet your child's needs.

Some organizations advocate that you write a detailed plan outlining what is to happen in each aspect of your child's life after your death. While it's a good idea to make your wishes clear, what if circumstances change? What if the agency you choose to deliver services to your child goes out of business? What if the government decides to close all group homes and move people into some other kind of living arrangement? What if your child just doesn't like it? What if he likes it when he's thirty but needs something different at fifty?

The environment in which human services operate is extremely volatile right now. Legislators are under increasing pressure to contain costs. Health care is targeted for some kind of reform, but no one seems to know when or how. In the meantime, advocates are bringing court cases to demand that services be provided in less and less restrictive environments. Who knows what services will look like in the next few years, let alone the next few decades? How will parents ensure that their children with disabilities take advantage of some of the changes and don't get lost in the shuffle?

Too many parents assume that people with cognitive disabilities are better off with their "own kind." Nothing could be further from the truth. People who are socially isolated are often unhappy and prime candidates for abuse. In addition, most people with cognitive disabilities learn best by modeling other people. Considering that many people with cognitive disabilities need to improve their social skills, does it make sense to put them into a large group of people who all have poor social skills? Absolutely not.

This book proposes that you go outside of the human services system to ensure that your child has a healthy and satisfying life after you are no longer around. It suggests that you put together a network of non-paid friends and advocates who are committed to helping protect your child, to ensuring that he gets high quality care, and to making changes in his lifestyle as his needs dictate. This is not to say that your child might not associate with others who have cognitive disabilities or receive some support and guidance from human services professionals. But the human services professionals will not be in control of the quality of your child's life. Your child and his friends will.

In the following pages, you will learn how to expand and deepen your child's relationships. You will also learn how to ask others to maintain their support of your child after your death. It's not another person-centered planning process; though it has some things in common with this new approach. This book offers a lot of very practical suggestions on how parents can take steps to ensure good lives for their children.

The information in the book was obtained through more than fifteen years of contact with families, service providers, and advocates in the disability field. People with disabilities are involved in their communities to a greater extent than ever before. The book includes dozens of sketches illustrating some of the many ways that people are networked. Details such as names and physical characteristics have been altered to protect the confidentiality of the people involved.

We'll take a brief look at your options for managing inheritance too, but there are other, more detailed publications that can help you decide how to leave money to your child. A list of some of these publications is included in Appendix A. By all means, if you can leave your child something, please do. As we all know, money can create some options for your child that might not be available otherwise. But please don't assume that just because you've got a will, your child has it made. As we've seen, money isn't everything.

CHAPTER **I**

WHAT AM I
GOING TO DO?

"The only thing I want out of life is for my child to die five minutes before I do."

❖

"Who's going to look out for her? No one is going to take care of her like I do."

❖

"Sure, people like them when they're little and cute, but no one seems to want to deal with them when they are grown up."

What parents want for their children with disabilities and what they get are often two completely different things. The government offices and private agencies responsible for serving them make for a huge, complicated system. Even those who work in this system agree that it seems to be an impersonal bureaucracy incapable of dealing with people as individuals. For example, people are typically fit into programs designed by the human services system, not designed for the individual. If there's a nursing home placement available and your child is in a wheelchair, she may end up in the nursing home even though it might not be the best place for her. If there's a group home placement available in a house of eight people, your child may end up there even if she would do better living with only one or two people. If your child needs only a few hours of supervision per week, and all that's available is a twenty-four-hour intensive program, she may end up there for lack of something better. Many times, such programs even seem to discourage contact with the outside world.

Even parents, at times, discourage other people from being involved with their child. They've bought societal messages that there is something wrong with being different, that their child needs to be with others like herself, and that other people don't want to deal with someone who has a disability. Mostly, however, parents have mixed feelings. They know what they want for their child in a general way, but don't know how to go about achieving it.

What parents and people with disabilities want from caretakers and the human service system is really pretty basic.

WHAT DO PEOPLE WANT?

People with disabilities and their parents want what everyone else wants. They want a life and all that means. In Pennsylvania, the state office of mental retardation publishes a document called *Everyday Lives*. The document is named for a quote by John McKnight, a national expert on community building:

> *"Our goal should be clear. We are seeking nothing less than a life surrounded by the richness and diversity of community. A collective life. A common life. An Everyday Life. A powerful life that gains its joy from the creativity and connectedness that comes when we join in association as citizens to create an inclusive world."*

According to the *Everyday Lives* booklet, people with mental retardation want the following things:

- **Choice** - in the decisions of life; choice of jobs, friends, recreation, where and with whom to live.
- **Control** - of relationships, money, transportation, services, medicine, and staff.
- **Permanency** - with a life in the community among family and friends; no fear of returning to the institution.
- **Security** - and protection for those who have difficulty in communication; competent services; and safety in the community.
- **Freedom** - of movement, and from stigma.
- **Prosperity** - freedom from poverty and a chance to be successful.
- **Individuality** - by having a name and a personal history and by making a difference; having dignity and status.
- **Relationships** - with friends, family, and partners.
- **Recognition** - of abilities, capacities, and gifts.
- **Privacy** - of records, files, and histories; protection from being labeled and the option of living alone.
- **Citizenship** - as part of the community, having a feeling of connectedness, partnership in dreams and beliefs; playing a part in decisions which affect you.
- **Passion** - in advocates and self-advocates to fight and dream together.

For another view of what people with disabilities want, look at the list in the box on pages 4–5, which was compiled in 1985 by People First of Washington. People First is a self-advocating group comprised entirely of people with developmental disabilities. They stress that what they want does not require money, new laws, rules, or regulations. They want staff to see people with disabilities as valuable and competent people.

WHAT WE WANT FROM RESIDENTIAL PROGRAMS

1. Programs that help us get out into the community so we can have the same experiences as other people.

"programs that take people places 1 to 1 and not in large groups"

"programs that encourage us to do things outside of the place where we live"

2. Programs that let us and help us to make good choices and be responsible.

"programs that give people choices about where they live and how many people they live with"

"programs that allow and expect people to make their own decisions, be responsible and look after themselves"

"programs that allow people to make their own choices about marriage and sexual matters"

3. Programs that encourage and assist us in developing independence.

"programs that teach us new things and not the same old thing over and over again"

The Parent's Role

And what do parents want? Today, many parents want to know that their child will be happy and secure after the parents die. Parents want to be assured that their children can experience and enjoy all those things described in the *Everyday Lives* document: recognition, relationships, permanency, etc.

Unfortunately, many programs, particularly residential, are unable to meet the expectations of people with disabilities and their parents. This is due primarily to their need to set rules and procedures to manage large numbers of people and their obligation to operate according to governmental and business guidelines.

Unless your child dies before you do, this means you must figure out how to guarantee a fulfilling existence for your son or

"programs that treat people like 'you can!' and not like
'you can't'"

4. **Respect. Respect and dignity are very important. Without respect, dignity, and a value for people none of
these other things will work.**
"programs that let us decide about activities, bedtime, etc."
"programs that don't have places that are 'off limits' or
'staff only'"
"programs that let us disagree without being afraid of
getting in trouble"

5. **A chance to meet and know a wide variety of people.**
"programs that help us meet people who are not
developmentally disabled"
"programs that help us to meet people who like the same
things we do"
"programs that help us get together with others in the
community"

daughter after your death. As discussed in the Introduction, this
book argues that the best way to achieve this goal may be to recruit friends who will volunteer the energy and attention needed
to ensure a good life for your child. The next sections explain why
this course of action may be better than more traditional ones.

THE LONG-TERM CARE CRISIS

The field of human services changes and evolves just like every other
field. A hundred years ago, people thought that people with cognitive
disabilities should be placed away from everyone else, on top of a hill
somewhere in an institution with "their own kind." Such "institutional services" were the service models of their day. Institutional
services were the state of the art, and people were placed in institu-

tions in droves. Doctors routinely told new parents to send their children with disabilities to institutions and forget about them.

In the last couple of decades, the United States has evolved its thinking about people with cognitive disabilities and decided that they are best served in "community services"—in programs situated within the general community, close to nondisabled people. People have been moving out of institutions at a steady rate for twenty years, evidence of the trend toward community supports. In fact, some states have closed their public institutions, opting instead to serve people in foster care, group homes, or with supports within their family's home.

With the exception of Nevada, all states have reduced their institutional populations since 1977. New Hampshire, the District of Columbia, Rhode Island, and Vermont are all now "institution free," meaning that these states no longer operate any public institutions for people with mental retardation. New Jersey and New York have announced plans to close their state-operated institutions. Several other states are rapidly transferring institutional residents to community living. (These statistics were published in the Fourth National Study of Public Spending for Mental Retardation and Developmental Disabilities in the United States, conducted by the University of Illinois at Chicago's Institute on Disability and Human Development, 1994.)

Unfortunately, phasing out institutional living in favor of community living has not turned out to be a cure-all. Long-term care as it exists today is undergoing a crisis. The original community service models of the last twenty-five years, such as group homes and sheltered workshops, are beginning to come under attack because of their intensive labor demands and their difficulties responding to individual needs. Residential service models are defined by the type of housing—congregate, small group, individualized; and the staffing patterns—such as twenty-four hour, or three residents to one staff; and the assumptions upon which the model is built—such as the medical model (people are sick and need to be cured), or the humanistic model (people's dignity and intrinsic value are most important). More details about residential services currently available are provided in Chapter 10.

Labor problems and inflexibility are not the only problems with current residential options. Evidence is also strong that many people with cognitive disabilities are being abused in these types of services, many more than were originally thought. Abuses range from emotional to physical, from neglect to the conscious, intentional inflicting of harm. As part of my work as a professional advocate for people with mental retardation, I represented many people who were abused while living in residential programs, either by other residents or staff members. Included among the many people I saw were a young man who was burned several times with cigarettes, an older woman who was raped twice, and a young boy who was kept in a locked box when he acted inappropriately. Unfortunately, these cases weren't unusual. There were several advocacy offices like mine throughout the country, all with more abuse cases than we could handle.

How can the social service system, which was originally designed to help people, turn out to be harmful? There is no doubt that tremendous strides have been made by social services on behalf of people with disabilities. People are living longer, media images and societal perceptions have dramatically improved, and we know more about what kind of supports people need than ever before. The problem starts when the social service system begins to control the lives of the people it is designed to serve. When paid strangers begin to have control over the life of a person with disabilities, the decisions that are made unfortunately won't always be in the person's best interest. It's this control that makes it difficult for people to lead natural, happy, and productive lives.

What Exactly Is Going Wrong?

In his book, *Crossing the River: Creating a Conceptual Revolution in Community and Disability*, David Schwartz discusses five problem areas in human services for people with disabilities.

1. Abuse, neglect, and psychotropic (mood altering) drug use - Schwartz notes that there is evidence of at least some abuse and neglect of people in group homes, workshops, recreation programs, and other community services. He describes reports that people with disabilities have made about staff abuse. He reports that psychotropic drugs such as Haldol and Melaril are being used at dosages high enough to modify the behavior of people in residential programs—dosages high enough to warrant further investigation. Alarmingly, Schwartz points out that the community system was designed to solve these very problems. The institutions had the same problems years ago and when people were moved into community residences, concerted efforts were made to reduce the use of drugs. Now, it is possible that more drugs are being used in the community than in institutions. While community settings are vastly superior to institutions, these are troubling problems to find.

2. A staff "retention and recruitment" crisis - Schwartz refers to the constant turnover of staff in community residential settings. He points out that constant changes in staff put a dramatic burden on people living in the residence. Over and over again, residents are forced to develop new relationships with the people who take care of their most intimate needs. It's hard to have a stranger come in to help you with things such as bathing, toileting, or even managing money. More information on the staffing crisis is included later in this chapter under the section "Staffing Problems."

3. Isolation of people served - Schwartz discusses the paradox of community settings: they were thought to be a major improvement over institutions because they would increase contact between typical members of the community and people with disabilities. Unfortunately, it seldom works this way. Studies have found that people with disabilities in community settings have many fewer relationships than nondisabled people. And staff members and other people with disabilities represent the majority of their acquaintances. This does not reflect typical community life and can lead to major concerns for the well-being of people with mental retardation.

4. Increasing clinicalization of the field - Here Schwartz describes the over-application of technological concepts to human problems and the tendency to forget about the person in the midst of all this analysis. Schwartz gives the example of seeing an elderly man tied to a wheelchair, crying out "Help me, help me." An overly clinical view of the man's behavior would be that it is "inappropriate attention seeking behavior" and the professional's response would be to ignore him for fear of "positively reinforcing" the inappropriate behavior. Looking at the man in the wheelchair as a person, you see that he is really crying out for help, though it may not be obvious at first what type of help he wants. A humanistic response would be to identify and meet his need, not to ignore him.

5. Retarding effects of the system itself upon those dependent upon it - In other words, the community system of residential and day programs can limit the opportunities people with disabilities have for realizing their full potential. Most notably, Schwartz discusses how difficult it is for workers to move from the sheltered workshop system into real work opportunities.

Perhaps much of the dissatisfaction with the residential system that people with cognitive disabilities and their families feel can be best expressed through "You and I," the poem on page 10 written by Elaine Popovich of Lutheran Social Services.

Relying On Service Models

"I chose the private institution for my child's placement after I die. It's been there a hundred years and seems like the most permanent option."

"I think the group home sounds ideal for her. There's a waiting list, but if I could just get her into one, our worries would be over."

"First they told us to institutionalize her. Then group homes were all the rage. Now, they're talking about some kind of foster care arrangement. What's next? We're not talking about some social experiment here, we're talking about my daughter."

The human service system is constantly trying to advance the state of the art in providing supports to people with disabilities. Human services are not static, inert things by any means. The problem is

You and I

I am resident. You reside.

I am admitted. You move in.

I am aggressive. You are assertive.

I have behavior problems. You are rude.

I am noncompliant. You don't like being told what to do.

When I ask you out for dinner, it is an outing.
When you ask someone out, it is a date.

I do not know how many people have read the
progress notes people write about me. I don't even know
what is in there. You didn't speak to your best friend
for months after they read your journal.

I make mistakes during my check-writing program. Some day
I might get a bank account. You forgot to record some withdrawals from
your account. The bank called to remind you.

I wanted to talk with the nice-looking person behind us at the grocery store.
I was told that it was inappropriate to talk to strangers.
You met your spouse in the produce department.
They couldn't find the bean sprouts.

I celebrated my birthday yesterday with five other residents and
two staff members. I hope my family sends a card.
Your family threw you a surprise party.
Your brother couldn't make it from out of state.
It sounded wonderful.

My case manager sends a report every month to my guardian.
It says everything I did wrong and some things I did right.
You are still mad at your sister for calling your mom
after you got that speeding ticket.

I am on a special diet because I am 5 pounds over my ideal body weight.
Your doctor gave up telling you.

I am learning household skills. You hate house work.

I am learning leisure skills. Your shirt says you are a "couch potato."

After I do my budget program tonight, I might get to go to
McDonald's if I have enough money. You were glad that the new French
restaurant took your charge card.

My casemanager, psychologist, R.N., occupational therapist,
physical therapist, nutritionist and house staff set goals for me for next year.
You haven't decided what you want out of life.

Some day I will be discharged . . . maybe.
You will move onward and upward.

that parents of people with disabilities are often told that one particular *service model*, or type of program, is "the answer"—that the service model will provide security, safety, and happiness for the rest of that child's life. The reality is that service models are not panaceas. They have frequently changed in the 150 years or so that energy has been focused on helping people with cognitive disabilities. Even if service models were stable, dependable things, quality of life is not. Just because someone lives in an institution that has been around for a hundred years does not mean that she is living a good life.

Staffing Problems

"I feel really good about Stephen's situation. He has Mrs. Kay to look after him. She's a wonderful woman who's always doing extra things for the kids."

Some truly wonderful people work in the human service system. Many times they are extraordinarily dedicated folks committed to stressful but meaningful work. Direct care staff, as they are often called, are frequently stretched to the limits. In many places, they are called upon to be nurturers, recreational activity aides, counselors, behavior management specialists, etc. In group home environments, they are often required to be cooks, budget managers, van drivers, home repair experts, nutritionists, you name it. Small wonder that the people talented enough to do all these jobs quickly get kicked upstairs to teach other people how to do it or are just biding their time until something more lucrative comes along.

Staff turnover is a major problem. Some areas estimate that turnover occurs at the rate of 100 percent, meaning that each position will be filled by a different person every year. There are many reasons for the exceptionally high rate of turnover, including low pay, extremely varied demands, difficult hours, weekend and holiday duty, and the low status of the position. Higher level positions turn over at a slower rate, but it is still rare to see a supervisor who has been in the same position for more than five years in most privately run community service enterprises.

The effects of turnover on people with disabilities are disturbing. They are often socially isolated to begin with. They rely on staff for all their social contact. Staff are their friends, their companions, even their surrogate parents. Then staff members leave for other jobs and are never seen again. The person with the disability goes through a grieving process which goes unrecognized. Residential program providers in Pennsylvania described the effect of high turnover on people living in their facilities in the following ways:

> "This disruption in our residents' lives is not something most of them understand and hence results in a traumatic experience for them emotionally and mentally."
>
> ❖
>
> "In the MR field, it will often take anywhere from one month to a year for our clients to become accustomed to new staff. This most often leads to confusion and behavior problems."
>
> ❖
>
> ". . . the large turnover in direct care positions creates a very tentative relationship with clients who need as much stability as possible. Clients are cautious about forming close trusts, knowing that staff members may not be employed at that particular agency for very long."
>
> ❖
>
> ". . . residents who are used to these staff lose them and for every staff lost, the residents have an adjustment period."
>
> ❖
>
> "The clients are the ones who get hurt the most. They need to feel comfortable and it is hard when people keep changing."

The same study, conducted by the Pennsylvania Legislative and Budget Finance Committee, included a statement from a thirteen-year-old who lived in one of the facilities surveyed. The teenager described her frustration at not having time to play games, a lack of affection from caregivers, and insufficient attention to her physical needs, such as being re-positioned often enough.

Later in the study, a provider of residential care talks about the impact of staff shortages on family members as well as the people living in the facilities. The provider noted that staffing problems were so severe that parents of residents were called to take their children back on weekends, and they often had to move all the residents who were left into as few group homes as possible to minimize staffing requirements. The provider said that all this moving around upset residents and promoted behavior problems. The provider said that it was difficult to ensure the safety of the residents and the staff in such a situation.

This provider's concerns about safety were echoed by at least one other:

> *"As providers, we must frequently respond to situations in which our clients are put in jeopardy because of unqualified staff or exhausted staff. . . ."*

Unfortunately, having such intense feelings of loss every year is simply too much to deal with. As a result, the person with the disability often does one of two things: learns not to form deep attachments to staff people, thereby having essentially no one in her life to love, or becomes dysfunctional because of the madness of trying to deal with the situation.

Even if your child is fortunate enough to be blessed with highly stable staff, staff don't live forever and no one has the same level of commitment to a paid relationship that they have for relationships they freely choose. Staff are also subject to the demands of management and government regulations. If more paperwork is required, staff are going to do it at the expense of time with your son or daughter.

Romanticizing the Community

It's important to state up front what we all know—community living isn't perfect. There is a real danger in assuming that if we can just get people with disabilities more involved in society, everything will be perfect. The truth is, many of our neighborhoods are deteriorating. Not too many people have a true sense of "belonging" to a neighborhood anymore. Crime seems to be constantly increasing, eroding our sense of safety and comfort. Chances are, as people with disabilities become more involved in community life, they too will share our concerns about crime and the decline of neighborhood life. Sometimes, people with disabilities move out of institutions into an apartment of their own, truly free for the first time in their lives. And they are very, very lonely.

Does any of this mean that people with disabilities should remain segregated away from us? Absolutely not. Our focus has to be on evolving society to the point where it fully supports each member's unique contributions and gifts. We need to move toward a healthier society for all of us, one that makes us all feel safe and included.

PLANNING FOR THE FUTURE

In addition to concerns about society in general, parents often have strong fears about the future of their child with disabilities. Dealing with the idea of someone else taking care of your child is never easy. Though most children grow up and leave home, this process is always complicated and emotionally charged. Parents are afraid that their child's skills aren't adequate preparation for the world. In addition, planning for their child's long-term care brings parents face to face with their own mortality, which is difficult for many people. Combined with all that, there is a feeling that no one will ever love your child the way you do and that no one will ever care for your child the way you do. Maybe the new caregiver will not understand your child's needs or be able to comfort her. How will she survive without her primary advocates, Mom and Dad? We've all seen what happens to people that no one cares about. What if no one cares about my kid?

> *"I've taken care of a lot of that. I've written out a very specific plan that will guide what my child is supposed to get at each stage of her life. If I die, all they have to do is follow the plan and she'll be well taken care of."*

Plans are only plans. Some of the assumptions you used in developing your plans may not be factors when it comes time to put that particular part of your plan into effect. There are probably thousands of examples of parents' plans not being followed because of some unforeseen circumstance. For example, what if you decide you want your child to live in a particular agency's group home and that agency goes out of business? What if public money dries up and the government says they can't pay for the placement? What if they discover a much better way to provide residential programming? What if your child hates her housemates?

What about your child's needs twenty-five years from now? Is it truly possible to predict what kind of services will be needed? What if she develops a physical disability and needs different supports? What if she really blossoms in the setting and decides she wants to move out on her own?

I think it's a good idea to get ideas about the future down on paper, but I think it's a mistake to assume that a document is going to be able to watch over your child for the rest of her life. Too much can go wrong.

So the question is—how can we see that our child with disabilities is happy, secure, and living in a situation that meets her needs for the rest of her life? How can we make sure that the environment changes with her as she ages and as her perceptions of what she wants change? It doesn't seem possible to write a plan that takes all these factors into account. Is it even plausible to write some kind of prescription for our child that is supposed to dictate how she will live for twenty or sixty years beyond our deaths? And if we write a plan that describes the type of program we want her to live in and the activities we want her to participate in, is that going to be enough to keep her safe?

Wouldn't it be much better if she were cared for by people who know and love her, people who have some sense of her history, people who are committed to her for the long haul? Wouldn't it be better if she were cared for by someone with whom she feels comfortable, someone with whom she can talk when she has a problem? People with cognitive disabilities need consistency in their relationships. You don't get that kind of long-term commitment from paid staff. People with cognitive disabilities need advocates who won't be swayed by budget crunches or lured away by better jobs. People with disabilities, just like everyone else, need to be loved just because of who they are. Being loved by someone who is being paid to love and care for you is not the same thing.

I am convinced that the best answer is to rely on other people. What your child needs is a supportive, caring group of advocates who *want* to look out for her after you're gone.

CHAPTER **2**

WHAT CAN
I COUNT ON?

There is only one resource I know of that is capable of making sure someone is happy and se-
cure, is responsive to changing trends and laws, and is able to fight
for changes when they are needed. That resource is other people.

It's true that people are not 100 percent reliable either, but
it's the only option that seems capable of meeting all the needs
we've discussed. People who give their time freely to your child
dramatically improve your child's chances of being well cared for
and happy. Consider the following scenarios:

> Donald used to live in an institution. His mother
> became dissatisfied with the care he was receiving
> and organized a group of supporters to look into
> alternative residences. She found eight people who
> agreed to help her with the project, including her
> neighbor, her minister, and Donald's sister. The
> group decided that Donald was able to live in a
> group home, despite his autism and his periodic

"outbursts." They put a lot of pressure on the county government and the institution and, after two years of fighting, Donald moved into a group home. His outbursts decreased, his health improved, and he began to smile a lot more. Members of his support group continued to visit Donald after he moved. Occasionally, everyone would get together to discuss his future.

Then, Donald's mother died. Her neighbor took over the group, making sure everybody got together regularly and recruiting new members as Donald's needs dictated. Suddenly, Donald began to have outbursts again. The group found out that someone new had moved into the house and that Donald and the new guy didn't get along. The group tried to get the group home staff to move the guy out again, but the staff refused. Finally, the group decided that Donald should live in a smaller group home with only one other person and some support staff. They lobbied hard for this, eventually winning. Donald now lives with someone he really likes and has 24-hour staff support. He hasn't had an outburst for five years. The neighbor still gets the group together; now they are working on getting Donald a job that he would like.

❖

Bill's son, Richard, is labeled "moderately handicapped." Bill decided that he could not rely on the human service system to set up an appropriate living situation for Richard, so he took matters into his own hands. Bill took out a long-term lease on an apartment in a highrise building in the city near public transportation. Using his business contacts, he found Richard a job bagging groceries in a nearby grocery store. Richard moved in to the apartment about six months ago and Bill stayed with him for a week teaching him how to use public transportation. Bill's biggest concern is Richard's inability to balance his checkbook. Bill recruited an accountant friend of his who agreed to meet with Richard monthly to help him with his checkbook and to annually file his taxes.

A few weeks ago, the doorman to Richard's building stopped Bill as he was leaving. The doorman told Bill that he noticed some unsavory characters following Richard as he walked from the bus stop one night. The doorman scared the men off and now makes sure to watch out for Richard every night as he gets off the bus. Bill thanked the doorman profusely and said that he felt bad that Richard was creating extra work for him. The doorman denied that it was extra work and said that he really enjoyed Richard. Bill feels that when he dies, Richard will be in good shape. Richard doesn't really need much more in the way of support; he makes friends easily and will continually broaden his network. By the time Bill dies, Richard will be accustomed to his new lifestyle, and his friends, like the doorman and the accountant, will be able to help him over any rough spots.

❖

Joanne has multiple disabilities, including a severe seizure disorder. She lives with a foster family. The arrangements were made while her mother, Mary, was still alive. Mary started to have some health problems of her own and, after her husband died, realized that she would have difficulty lifting and bathing Joanne, who was still living at home. Mary applied for some home health care, asking for an aide to come to their home and assist with bathing and feeding Joanne. When that problem was solved, they began to look into residential options. A friend told them about the family living program, a type of foster care. It sounded like the best idea for Joanne, who liked being around people of all ages. Her mother wasn't too keen on group homes and felt that they weren't "cozy" enough.

Mary and Joanne were Quakers, so they went to their meeting's membership and asked if anyone would be interested in having Joanne move in with them. They explained that the cost of Joanne's care would be reimbursed by the government and that there were some paperwork requirements. (See the description of "Family Living" in Chapter 10.) Luckily, they found a family with a young stay-at-home mother who was interested in the extra income. After several visits back and forth, Joanne moved in. She saw her mother regularly until Mary's death, 10 months later. Because Mary involved the Quaker meeting in Joanne's search for a residence, the whole group now takes an interest in Joanne. Members of the Quaker meeting visit her, invite her on trips and assist when her new family needs something.

All three of the people with disabilities described above are living happy and secure lives. They are in settings which allow for growth, changing needs, and individuality. They are surrounded by friends who look out for them and try to help them solve problems as they come up.

Their lives are not perfect, of course. Richard's a little lonely and really wants a girlfriend. Fortunately, he lives in the community, which increases the likelihood that he will meet someone to date. He's also talked to his co-workers at the grocery store about the problem and they've agreed to make some introductions. All in all though, Richard's life is good.

Happy results like these aren't due to luck. They're due to a lot of energy and planning on the part of their families. While the situations are really different, there are some common denominators that are useful to identify:

1. Each individual's desires and needs were strongly considered in setting up the living arrangement.

2. Each person was involved in selecting where and how he was to live.

3. **Each person has a supportive group of friends who are not paid to be involved with them.**

4. **These friends maintain regular contact with the person and have a good sense of who that person is and what they need or want.**

5. **The friends are willing to step in and resolve problems as they arise.**

6. **There is more than one friend involved, providing back-up and mutual support.**

7. **Nobody assumed that the human service system was the absolute answer to their problem.** In fact, the families recognized the problems inherent in the human service system and set up safeguards to avoid them.

GETTING STARTED

No doubt, if Donald's mother and Mary were still alive, they would still be heavily involved with their children, troubleshooting problems as they come up and expanding their options in other areas like work or recreation. All three parents recognized that their children's lives were dynamic things. They have made it possible for friends to work on expanding those options simply by involving them in their child's life.

I suggest that you do the same. This book will help you with the nuts and bolts of finding friends devoted to your child and asking them to become intimately involved with the details of your child's life. First though, you need to have a vision of what your child's life will look like. You need to develop that vision with your child. Even if your child has severe disabilities you can still get an idea of his preferences in living situations. Does he like a lot of people around all the time or just a few? Does he like to spend time outside—maybe you want to look into something in the country? Does he like animals or no? Chances are you have some very definite ideas of your child's preferences despite the severity of his disability.

To get started, it may be helpful to write down your answers to the following questions:

What kind of residence would be best for your child? An apartment building with a nearby bus stop? A house in the country, away from dangerous streets? A place of his own, or a house with a big family with lots of activity and commotion?

Is there a particular geographic location that would be good? The neighborhood where your son grew up, or someplace where he has other relatives?

Is your child someone who gets along easily with others or not? How many people should he live with? How important is it that he like and get along with whomever he lives with?

What are his future plans for work? Does he want to work competitively? What would his day look like?

What about interests and hobbies? Budding painter, exceptional gardener. . . . Address how these activities would be nurtured and supported in your vision.

What about other leisure time? Does your child need time just to goof off, watch television, or whatever? Or does he benefit more from a lot of structured activities like choir practice on Monday, swimming at the Y on Tuesday, etc.?

After considering these ideas and getting your child's input, start sketching out what you and your child would like things to look like after you die. Be as detailed as you like, keeping in mind that this is just a vision, subject to changes and modifications. Once you are satisfied with what you have, you can start looking at the resources you need to make your vision a reality.

One thing that I ask is that you don't use any "human service jargon." Don't say, for example, "I want Joe to live in a group home and work in a sheltered workshop, maximizing his potential." Remember, this is a long-term vision—group homes and sheltered workshops may not be around twenty years from now. Who knows? Instead say things like:

> *"I want Joe to live in a house with one or two other men. I want him to be able to work in a situation that he can manage, bringing him into contact with other people on a regular basis. I want him to be able to continue his gardening. I want him to be surrounded by people who like him and care about him."*

You may find that your child's life doesn't seem rich enough or is too dependent on human service programs. You may also find that you don't really know what your child needs or wants to be happy and fulfilled. If so, you're in for a period of exploration and discovery. Your vision, for the moment, may look something like this:

"I want Joe to live with people that he really likes. I want him to explore more things so that he can find a job that he really likes. I want him to try out different hobbies so that he can better fill his time."

Many people with cognitive disabilities haven't had a chance to experience the world like typical people have. They have been sheltered away in special programs or well-meaning family members just wouldn't take them different places. It's perfectly acceptable to work on broadening your child's experiences before deciding on your vision for the future. In fact, if all you can come up with as a vision is a group home, the sheltered workshop, and the special bowling league on Saturday, I recommend some extensive exploration, beginning with a review of the information in Chapter 4. You and your child have a lot of options; it's simply a matter of who you know.

SUPPORTING YOUR CHILD'S VISION

Once you have sketched out at least a rough vision for your child's future, the next step is to figure out what kinds of friends can help your child realize that vision. Could one or two friends with a genuine interest in your child's well-being oversee his life in the community? For instance, could he live on his own if he had a friend in the same apartment building who checked on him once in a while? Or does he have more extensive needs, so that he might need a larger network of friends with different areas of expertise to help him out?

Use the checklist on the following pages to help you consider how much support your child might need from others. (If your child is not yet an adult, answer the questions based on how you expect him to be functioning by the time he is a young adult.)

SUPPORT CHECKLIST

Mark each of the following items according to this code:

I - Does independently
R - Needs reminders only
A - Needs more assistance
D - Needs someone else to do this

PERSONAL CARE

☐ Dressing
☐ Eating
☐ Brushing teeth
☐ Visiting doctor/dentist/etc.
☐ Getting haircut
☐ Using toilet

☐ Bathing
☐ Grooming
☐ Taking medicine
☐ Other _____
_____
_____

HOUSEKEEPING

☐ Vacuuming
☐ Cleaning kitchen
☐ Dusting
☐ Lawn care
☐ Replacing/Repairing items
☐ Sweeping/mopping

☐ Cleaning bathroom
☐ Making bed
☐ Washing dishes
☐ Other _____
_____
_____

MEAL PREPARATION

☐ Meal planning
☐ Follows recipes/instructions
☐ Uses appliances
☐ Cooks a variety of foods
   for all meals

☐ Shopping for groceries
☐ Maintains healthy diet
☐ Other _____
_____
_____

LAUNDRY/CLOTHING CARE

☐ Washes clothing
☐ Ironing
☐ Replaces clothes
☐ Stores clothing
   (hanging, folding, etc.)

☐ Uses dryer
☐ Mends/Repairs clothing
☐ Chooses clothes appropriately
☐ Other _____
_____
_____

TRANSPORTATION

- [ ] Drives
- [ ] Uses bus/train
- [ ] Uses cabs
- [ ] Gives addresses
- [ ] Makes overnight/travel arrangements
- [ ] Maintains vehicle
- [ ] Shares personal information
- [ ] Purchases tickets
- [ ] Other _____

_____

_____

FINANCES

- [ ] Budgets
- [ ] Purchases items from store
- [ ] Files taxes
- [ ] Manages bank account
- [ ] Manages government benefits
- [ ] Manages checkbook
- [ ] Shops wisely
- [ ] Other _____

_____

_____

RECREATION AND LEISURE

- [ ] Amuses self at home
- [ ] Uses community recreation facilities
- [ ] Gets transportation to recreation sites
- [ ] Joins classes/clubs
- [ ] Purchases recreational/ hobby items
- [ ] Other _____

_____

SAFETY

- [ ] Handles fire emergencies
- [ ] Avoids dangerous places/situations outside of the home
- [ ] Avoids dangerous situations within the home
- [ ] Deals with police/emergency personnel
- [ ] Manages medical emergencies
- [ ] Other _____

RELATIONSHIPS

- [ ] Makes new friends
- [ ] Maintains friendships
- [ ] Socializes appropriately
- [ ] Uses relationships to find answers to problems
- [ ] Practices safe sex/birth control
- [ ] Other _____

EMPLOYMENT
❑ Deals with boss/coworkers appropriately
❑ Identifies possible places of employment
❑ Makes application/interviews
❑ Uses employee benefits
❑ Punctual
❑ Other _____

The Support Checklist is not intended to be highly detailed. However, your answers to these questions should help you think more concretely about the vision for your child's future and what type of support may be needed. The list should be updated every five years or so (more often if your child is young). It's hard to predict how much anyone will grow, and you will most likely be surprised by your child's progress in five years.

You may notice some themes. For example, if your child mainly needs help with job-related issues, it might help to introduce him to a local mall manager or someone else with a lot of business connections. If "home economics" seems to be a problem, he may do well to be matched with a homemaker in the neighborhood. If he just needs advice once in awhile, he may need a friend he can call any time of the day or night with questions. Then again, your child may need a combination of these types of supports.

If your child is unable to handle many or most of these areas independently, you may want to consider this when thinking about residential options for him. For example, you may want to look for a living arrangement where trained staff can help your child learn to handle some of these responsibilities on his own, or can take care of the housekeeping, meal preparation, etc. for him. In other words, it would be difficult to find one or more people who would agree to help your child with *everything* on the list above free of charge, day in and day out, year after year.

Even if your son needs a residential program, however, he will still need some committed non-paid people in his life. In fact, he'll probably need them more because of his vulnerability and the amount of control that residential programs have over the lives of their residents. His friends can attend program planning meetings, visit frequently, etc. Even if total care is being provided for your child, he will always need to have some non-paid advocates looking out for him. (For more information on residential options currently available, and the types of supports available in each, see Chapter 10.)

It is important not to let the Support Checklist limit your thinking about relationships for your child. One of the worst things you can do is think of your child as a bundle of deficiencies and only recruit people who meet particular needs. It is also crucial to recruit others who will appreciate your child's strengths. Such relationships are more likely to be reciprocal and lasting. For more information on identifying your child's strengths, please refer to Chapter 4.

YOUR CHILD'S EXISTING NETWORK

Obviously, if your child already has friends who can help support him in the community, planning for his future will be a lot easier. Unfortunately, most people with disabilities have fewer social contacts than people without disabilities. To find out if this is true for your child, jot down your answers to the following questions:

1. How many people do I have in my own life?
   ✐ List all your friends, acquaintances, relatives, co-workers—everyone you know.

2. How many of these people are paid to spend time with me?
   ✐ Highlight or underline these relationships.

3. How many of these people are willing to help me out of a jam by giving me advice, sticking up for me, etc.?
   ✐ Put little stars by these people.

Now, do the same for your child, asking one additional question:

4. How many of these people also have a disability?

Most people find that their child knows far fewer people than they do themselves, or that the vast majority of their child's relationships are with people with disabilities or people who are paid to spend time with them. Usually there are relatively few people who do not fall into one of these two categories who are willing to stick up for them or support them through a crisis. The situation is exaggerated for people who live in residential programs. In one study, researchers found that 42 percent of people who lived in community programs had no personal friends or special relationships, while 83 percent had no contact with non-handicapped people whatsoever. The situation was even worse in state-run facilities, with 63 percent having no personal friends or special relationships and 96 percent having no social contact with non-handicapped people.

Fortunately, even if your child has relatively few friends now, that does not have to be a permanent situation. The next chapters explain how you can help him weave a strong and supportive network of friends.

CHAPTER 3

FIRST THINGS FIRST

People with cognitive disabilities are often limited in the options they have for their future. This can be due to their lack of relationships with nondisabled people or their lack of experience with what the world has to offer. Primarily, though, options are limited by people's perceptions. If you are perceived as being unathletic, you will probably not receive an athletic scholarship to college. Likewise, if you are perceived as "a burden," as many people with disabilities are, you probably will not have the same options for long-term living as the rest of us. Many negative images have been used in association with people with disabilities over the years. Parents, like the rest of society, learn to perceive all people with disabilities, including their children, in these ways.

Wolf Wolfensberger, a professor of sociology at Syracuse University, has identified several negative images commonly associated with people with disabilities, including:

- subhuman, e.g. animal, vegetable, or object
- menace to society, or at least an object of dread
- person to be pitied

      ✑ burden of charity, to be reluctantly supported
          (usually on a bare subsistence level) by other
          people in more valued roles
      ✑ a person who has not grown into maturity, perhaps
          never will, or has regressed back to the child level
      ✑ a holy innocent, unaware of good or evil, and
          incapable of doing wrong, perhaps in need of
          protection from a less pure society
      ✑ a sick or diseased organism

At first glance, these descriptions seem alien to today's perceptions of people with disabilities. Unfortunately, if you are listening with an ear for this type of thing, you can hear and see examples of this image casting from human service workers and families talking about people with disabilities. For example:

> *"My son, Robbie, is a victim of Down syndrome."*

This was said by a devoted parent when asked to describe her reason for volunteering at a social service agency. If you look at the description critically you can say that "Robbie" is being portrayed as a person to be pitied. When you consider that Robbie is a 25-year-old man, you could probably add that his mother views him as a person who has not grown into maturity. Most competent, contributing men would be called Rob, Bob, or Robert.

> *"I always give to the Jerry Lewis telethon. Somebody has to look out for those poor kids."*

A lot of people with disabilities are critical of the famous telethon. This is not just because of the low percentage of the money raised which actually reaches people in need but also because of the negative images portrayed. Critics feel that the telethon conveys images of people with disabilities as holy innocents and, again, objects of pity.

> *"It's a really great program. On Monday, Melanie has one hour of play therapy, and on Wednesday, all the kids get music therapy."*

Wolfensberger points out that people in programs often have fairly ordinary aspects of their lives described as a form of therapy. Adults who garden are engaged in "horticultural therapy" and children

who splash in wading pools are having "water therapy." This inclination to describe normal activities in this way portrays people as
sick or diseased. Who else needs "therapy"?

> *"We have eight kids living here. I love all my babies.*
> *Today, we're going to the bank and then out for pizza!"*

This was said by a well-meaning, enthusiastic human service worker
about the elderly people with mental retardation living in a group
home in which she worked. Because people with mental retardation are often viewed as children, many human service workers
describe them as "kids," "boys," or "girls" even when they are
older than the human service workers themselves.

> *"I don't want Suzanne to feel that she has to be saddled*
> *with looking out for Annie for the rest of her life. That's*
> *my burden, not hers."*

Annie, the person with the disability, is being described as
a burden of charity that the mother hopes to spare her other
daughter from having to shoulder. Many parents will talk about
the relationship between their children in such a way, not seeing
that such a relationship may actually be very positive for both
of their children.

One other example of creating negative images that
Wolfensberger cites is the tendency to place residential programs
near buildings or places with less than positive images. It really is
amazing how many group homes, for example, are located near
funeral parlors, trash dumps, hospitals, cemeteries, even slaughter
houses. Wolfensberger argues that such close proximity conveys
certain images—for example, that people with disabilities are trash,
or sick, or close to death. Wolfensberger cautions that there are
several ways negative or positive images can be conveyed and that
enlightened human service workers should take these methods
into account when setting up programs.

Dr. Wolfensberger has designed a training strategy that teaches
human service workers and interested others to see through some
of these strategies and identify more positive ways to serve people
with disabilities. One of the fundamental concepts is the self-ful-

filling prophecy. This is the idea that if you are perceived as dumb or cute or important, you will soon come to think of yourself as dumb, cute, or important and that you will soon begin to act accordingly. Goethe expresses a slightly different aspect of self-fulfilling prophecy below:

> *"If you treat an individual as he is, he will stay as he is, but if you treat him as if he were what he ought to be and could be, he will become what he ought to be and could be."*

To understand how all of this relates to the problem of long-term care for people with cognitive disabilities, consider this. If people with disabilities are considered to be valuable components of community life, they will have expanded options for long-term care. And parents who view their children as valuable and important will see and take advantage of more options for long-term care than those who are ashamed of their children or view them as burdens.

> *"I don't see my child as a burden to me. She's made my life what it is. I can't imagine my life without her. But other people are not going to see her the same way I do. I'm her mother. Every mother loves her child."*

It's hard to look at the negative images that Wolfensberger describes and think about how they affect people we love. It's harder still to recognize that you may have contributed to portraying people with disabilities in less than positive ways. It may also be difficult to see your child as you see other people. Parents shouldn't feel guilty about their part in stereotyping people with disabilities; they have had a lot of encouragement and support in doing so. Seeing people with disabilities as contributing, attractive members of society is a fairly recent phenomenon. In fact, parents who may have started out looking and talking about their children in more typical ways were probably discouraged from doing so by scores of professionals and other family members. For example, there are still physicians out there who advise parents of newborns with Down syndrome to institutionalize them, reasoning that they will never be able to walk, talk, or grow. It's a strong parent who can counter all of this pressure and continue to think of the child in more positive terms.

PARENTS NEED SUPPORT TOO

"Okay, I can see how I might need to do a better job of presenting my child to others. Not to be selfish, though, but I feel as if I need to take care of my own feelings first. I need to talk about the impact that having a disabled child has had on me. It was a shock when Beth was born. I didn't know anything about Down syndrome. My family didn't know what to do; they didn't even visit me in the hospital. I was a mess and I couldn't find anyone to support me. How am I supposed to cope with all this? People do see her those ways. It makes me mad, but they do."

Unfortunately, negative images do not just affect people with disabilities. They also are often transferred to those around them. Caregivers, including family members and paid staff, are sometimes looked down upon. People who don't know anything about disabilities may assume that family members have done something wrong or have some kind of illness that caused a disability.

If you are angry about the way others see you and your child, that's the first step to changing things. The next step is to find some like-minded parents of people with disabilities and get together to compare notes. A lot of very positive-thinking parents have told me that they don't think anyone else in the world would be able to understand them or give them the same kind of support that another parent of a child with a disability can. Let's face it, if you're not comfortable with the way people perceive you, it's going to be difficult to reach out to those people and change their perceptions about your child. By all means, if you feel the need to explore these issues, find a group or some friends and do so. For more information on groups that support parents and advocate for people with disabilities, please see Chapter 12.

CHANGING ATTITUDES

"I'd like to start changing some of these attitudes about people with disabilities, but it seems so overwhelming. I can't take on all of society. And it sounds as if all of society has to change its mind before my son is going to get the kind of program he needs."

There are a lot of little things you can do that will have an immediate effect on the people around you. To begin with, you need to identify the little things that can work to emphasize the "different-ness" of people with disabilities. These things can be changed fairly easily. Wolfensberger describes several ways that images of people with disabilities are affected. Those relevant to life at home with the family are described below:

Personal Impression. Is your child dressed like others of the same age who do not have disabilities? If not, this can be a red flag that signals her "different-ness" to others. I once noticed that a group home was dressing its residents in brightly colored, matching sweatpants and sweatshirt every day, even when the guys went to work. Nobody else on the job dressed in such a way and it wasn't difficult to figure out that the staff had probably done this because such clothing is inexpensive, and you don't have to fuss with zippers and belts and things. There are other options for easy dressing though, which would have minimized the differences between the men with the disabilities and their co-workers.

As a parent, you should pay particular attention to whether your child's clothes are age appropriate. I've met parents who dressed their adult children in young, child-like outfits. And I've also seen people with disabilities who were dressed just like their parents who were twenty to forty years older, complete with haircuts and glasses to match. The goal here is to look at a popular, productive person of your child's age and try to assist her in dressing and styling her hair like that person.

Grooming is also an issue. It's not unusual, sadly, to see a family spend money on braces for a nondisabled child, and ignore the crooked teeth of a child with disabilities. Good dental care, regular bathing, shaving—all of the elements of good grooming— are as important for people with disabilities as for people without disabilities.

Personal Possessions. Is your child's room like that of a typical person the same age? Or is it decorated in a much younger fashion? Hopefully, if you have a young child, she'll have guests for sleep-overs. What are the other kids going to think? Will they decide it's a great room or will they think your daughter is someone to be babied? If your child is an adult living in a group home, what does the living room look like? Is it mature and reflective of her tastes? How about other items such as lunch boxes, jewelry, and reading material? I once knew a man with mental retardation who rode the bus every day and was being subjected to some teasing. He and I couldn't figure out why the other people on the bus were calling him "retard." He dressed well, didn't talk on the bus, and didn't have any distinctive physical characteristics that might stigmatize him. We were both depressed about the situation and I was looking for something encouraging to say to him as he was getting ready to get on the bus one morning. I looked at him and saw that he had a "Special Olympics" ski cap in his hand ready to put on as he went out the door. Aha! I went out that day and bought him a new ski cap. Unfortunately, the teasing didn't end until the other riders stopped taking that particular bus, but it didn't happen to him again.

Activities and Activity Timing. One of the best ways to overcome prejudice is by bringing people into contact with each other. After months of seeing Ella at church, for example, people no longer viewed her as "mentally retarded with aggressive tendencies." They simply viewed her as Ella who had a lot of trouble dealing with being separated from her family. The point is, if you bring people into contact with each other, they will begin to see each other as individuals, not as stereotypes.

As a parent, you need to ask yourself whether your child's activities are typical of those engaged in by others of the same age. Do they occur at the same times and in the same locations? For example, many people with mental retardation like to bowl and do it well. Unfortunately, they are often relegated to bowling in "retarded bowling leagues," only going to the lanes at odd hours when there are no nondisabled bowlers around. I have also heard it said that some exceptional athletes are doomed to compete only in Special Olympics because they happen to have a disability label. This area seems to be the hardest for parents to grasp when looking to revitalize their child's image. In reality, many times only minor accommodations are needed for the person to go to the local YMCA, church, or community center to engage in some activities with people who do not have disabilities. Accommodations can range from a modified curriculum or project, to attending with a good friend who can act as a support, to just getting over your own apprehension about the process.

If your child has some friends with disabilities that she likes to visit occasionally, that's okay. What you need to do is look at the relationships you listed in Chapter 2. What's the balance between nondisabled friends and disabled friends? As mentioned before, most people with disabilities don't have enough contact with nondisabled people who are not paid to be with them. If this is not a problem for your child—great. If it is, chances are you can do some easy things to broaden your child's contacts. Let's suppose that your child is in a special bowling league and has a great time with some friends there. Why not schedule another bowling excursion with two or three friends at times there are non-disabled bowlers present? If she's pretty good, why not sign her up for a "normal" league? Why not allow her to practice her swimming skills from Special Olympics at the local community pool during regular hours?

The Relationship between the Person and Her Caregivers. You can learn a lot about people by listening to them talk to each other. In an article called "Toxic Talk," written for all parents, H. Norman Wright identifies "poison darts" that parents often throw at their children. These include sarcasm, hurtful teasing, subtle put-downs, reminding the child of misbehavior, expressing joy in the child's discipline ("serves you right, you brat"), projecting failure on the child ("I knew that you wouldn't be able to do it, it's too much for you"), taking cheap verbal shots at the child, verbally kicking the child when she's down, verbal harassment, broadcasting the child's humiliation, belittling, blaming, and fault finding. One that I might add is excessive pampering of the child, which I have seen often with parents of people with disabilities ("Don't worry about your coat, sweetie, Mommy will hang it up for you.")

While it is impossible to be respectful all the time in all situations, you may want to be particularly careful when in public. Remember, not only can you hurt your child's self-image, but you can also influence those around you into seeing your child as less than competent and less than desirable.

Allow for Individuality

As important as it is to figure out whether different aspects of your child's image may be keeping her from getting to know other people, it is important to allow for some individuality too. I have a very good friend, Frankie, who has cerebral palsy. In the beginning, I would occasionally suggest little ways of boosting her image, such as upgrading to a Gucci backpack or losing the neon green tights. Frankie was pretty resistant to these suggestions and justifiably so. She felt that it was her right as an adult to wear whatever she wanted and things like neon green tights were an expression of her personality. She's right too. She has the soul of an artist, is very whimsical, and a lot of fun. She has no lack of friends and manages her relationships very well. When I think of Frankie, I picture her in those green tights—she wouldn't be Frankie without some kind of whimsical fashion statement. So use these ideas judiciously. If your child clings to some aspect of her image, fine. The rest of us will adapt.

Empowerment

Of course, how your child conducts herself is going to have a major impact on her image. A lot of people feel that people with disabilities have been given negative messages about their self-worth and their autonomy. The results sometimes are people who are so eager to please that they're annoying, or people who get so angry they're dangerous.

Growing numbers of parents and professionals feel that such problems can be solved simply by empowering people to make their own choices about the way they live. As discussed in earlier chapters, many residential programs are felt to be too controlling. The person residing there never gets to choose what to eat, what to wear, or even how to spend the time between 5 and 6 o'clock in the evening. If one of eight residents has to go to the doctor, they all have to go. No matter what. Small wonder a lot of people with disabilities cope by becoming either aggressive or overly compliant.

If you are concerned that your daughter may need to take better charge of her own life, you can start to build her confidence in small ways. Let her choose her own clothing, control the TV remote, decide what the entire family will do on a particular Saturday. Take her with you when there are meetings where she will be discussed. Encourage her to speak up on her own behalf if she can. Always address questions to her when someone asks you in front of her. I do this whether the person can speak or not. You can develop a knack for making it seem smooth. It's also surprising to note how much a non-verbal person can communicate when invited to do so.

If your child does have communication difficulties, finding ways around them can go a long way to empowering her. If she is still in school, speech and language goals should definitely be given high priority in her Individualized Education Program (IEP). If she is receiving speech therapy, you should work closely with the therapist to make sure she is making as much progress as possible. Regularly let the therapist know your concerns and ask what you can do at home to help your child's communication skills. Don't allow your child to languish at the same skill level for months or years at a time. If your child never seems to reach her speech and language goals, let the therapist know that you (and, undoubtedly, your child) are frustrated. Perhaps your child needs different goals, a different plan of attack, or a different therapist.

If speech remains difficult or impossible for your child, investigate assistive communication devices and systems. These can include communication devices as simple as photo boards or as complex as talking communication systems with eye-gaze controls.

The entire field of assistive technology is growing tremendously. If it's been awhile since you and your child looked into what devices are available to give someone more control over their environment, check again. Many new products have become readily available, from voice-input computers to specially adapted toys. Your state departments of rehabilitation and education may be able to help point you in the right direction. So, too, can a speech-language pathologist.

If your child's communication style or abilities are different from other people's, this will, of course, have an effect on her image. For example, if she uses a talking communication device, some people will find that intriguing and others will think it's strange. Or if her speech is slow and slurred, some people will feel they don't have the time to hear her out, while others will admire her for trying so hard to express herself.

Bear in mind that being judged on how you communicate goes with the territory—for everyone, not just people with disabilities. Some people always make snap judgments about other people based on how they talk. For example, some people make assumptions about speakers who have Southern accents or New York accents or about men with relatively high-pitched voices. One thing is certain, however: your child will make a lot more friends if she makes an effort to communicate as well and as clearly as she can than if she doesn't make any effort at all.

Besides having difficulties with the mechanics of communication, people with disabilities sometimes have trouble speaking up. While I usually recommend that parents avoid segregated groups of people with disabilities when networking their child, I think self advocacy organizations are an exception. Such groups, comprised almost entirely of people with disabilities, are often effective in making your child feel comfortable in speaking her own mind and clarifing how she feels about her disability. If your daughter has issues of this nature, a self advocacy group may be a good place for her to begin exploring them. For more on self advocacy groups, see Chapter 12.

Empowerment is not just a buzz word. As you begin to help your child expand her social networks, you will most likely see her become more self-confident and empowered. She'll open up more, voice her opinion more often, and hopefully develop a comfortable style of relating. The sooner she starts having more contact with nondisabled people, the more you'll see her grow.

CHAPTER 4

HOW DO I HELP
DEVELOP RELATIONSHIPS
FOR MY CHILD?

To improve the likelihood of finding someone who will take a lifelong interest in your child, you need to match him with as many different people in as many different environments and situations as you can. These prospective friends should be non-paid, or give of their time freely.

It is okay to start out with someone who is engaged with your child in some professional way, if you feel the relationship will eventually become a true friendship. For example, your son's softball coach may seem to take a special interest in him, or a relationship with a camp counselor may become really special. Parents sometimes succeed in developing these types of relationships into something more. Just don't get trapped into thinking that the only people who will ever care about your child are human service workers. While it is often desirable or essential to have paid human service workers or staff involved with your child, there are limitations to paid relationships, as discussed in Chapter 1.

> *"This may sound mean or like I'm downgrading my child, but why would people want to be involved with him? He needs a lot of help and sometimes he can be a real pain. We still get looks in the grocery store when we go out. Who's going to want to take him places?"*

People want to be involved with other people, including people with disabilities, for many reasons, not the least of which is common interests. Think about the ways you made many of your friends. Maybe you both joined Weight Watchers at the same time or you both like a certain kind of music. It can and should be the same kind of process for people with disabilities. Follow your interests and the friends should come. We're going to talk more about how to do this later in this chapter.

The attraction of one person to another is a mystery that has fascinated people for decades. When I look at the friends I have, it's hard to say why we fit so well together. Why have some relationships lasted since I was a child and others just faded away? What is it about me that these people want in their lives? Why do I care about them? Ask yourself these questions. Friendship is a difficult thing to quantify. One thing seems certain though—it is a mutual thing. I give something to them and I receive something in return. Citizen advocates working with people with disabilities call this concept "reciprocity."

So the question becomes "what does my child have to give?" This can be harder to answer than it appears at first glance. Many parents have years of experience of meeting annually with human service professionals or educators to develop program plans for the upcoming year for their child. While this practice is undergoing some changes in some areas, it usually consists of looking at the individual's strengths and weaknesses and then developing strategies focusing on the weaknesses. Because of all this attention on the weaknesses, the strengths are often just token concepts. Through these types of meetings, professionals have taught us to think of our children in terms of their deficiencies, not their gifts. It can be hard to switch your thinking around.

Wolf Wolfensberger wrote a paper called "Common Assets of Mentally Retarded People That Are Commonly Not Acknowledged" which discusses gifts that many people with mental retardation possess. If you are wondering what your child has to offer in a relationship, Wolfensberger's list of assets may help you to see your child in another light. They include:

1. Heart qualities. Wolfensberger suggests that, because of their less than full intellectual development, many people with metal retardation have continued to develop their capacity for giving love and warmth to other people. He points out that for a variety of reasons many people with traditional intellectual development have had their heart qualities "choked out" of them.

2. Natural and positive spontaneity. Here Wolfensberger discusses a refreshing lack of attention to social convention. The best example I can think of to illustrate this point is the way people with mental retardation dance. There's no "I don't know the latest steps" or "what will these people think of me." They just dance if they want to. I also went to a karaoke bar one night and some people with mental retardation were there. It took no time at all for one of them to decide to sing. She broke the ice for everyone else and everyone had so much fun that we passed a hat to pay for an extra hour of the karaoke.

3. Generous, warm, and quick response to human contact, encouragement, and approval. It's relatively easy to make friends with a person with mental retardation.

4. A strong tendency to relate to the "heart qualities" of other people as opposed to their position or status. In other words, people with mental retardation usually relate to someone as kind or mean, upbeat or depressing, as opposed to whether or not they're unemployed or a U.S. Senator.

5. Genuine concern for things being well in the world. People with mental retardation are often truly distressed when they hear of problems that others are having, either next door or on another continent.

6. A greater capacity for unconditional love, i.e. complete, unqualified love, than many non-retarded people, probably because of the aforementioned qualities.

7. Trust. Many people with mental retardation have a tremendous ability to trust other people. Sometimes parents worry that their child may trust the wrong people, which is a concern, but the ability to trust is still a wonderful gift in its own right.

8. A lack of materialism and possessiveness. This may be due to the fact that many people with mental retardation do not have much money or it could be because of the development of heart qualities.

9. The ability to call forth tolerance, patience, and gentleness from other people. I witnessed this myself when I supported a man with mental retardation through a difficult workshop focusing on personal philosophy and values. The exercises were conducted in small groups and were highly intellectual. It was common for group members to become hostile with one another, but our group had no such problems. I think it was due to Ray's presence. Plus, in the course of having to break down complicated ideas so that he could understand them, we all came away with a strong understanding of the material.

10. Unfettered enjoyment of life's pleasures, including the simple ones. Wolfensberger points out that many nondisabled people have to take trips to the Caribbean or buy things to have fun, but that many people with mental retardation like being with friends, cooking, going out for ice cream, etc., in addition to more extravagant pleasures.

11. A tendency to be direct and concretely honest. In return, people with mental retardation expect that others will be honest with them.

12. A tendency to follow an issue, development, or idea in a rigorous, concrete sequentiality to its logical conclusion. I know a woman with mental retardation, Leeann, who sits on the board of directors of a local non-profit agency. She was told that there was a job description for board members. Leeann repeatedly asked for the job description, and once specific responsibilities were identified, set out to accomplish the tasks. Other board members said they appreciated Leeann's attention to the job description and that it helped them focus on their own roles better.

13. Less of a tendency to become bored than non-retarded people.

14. Unlikely to be misled, sidetracked, or confused by clever but erroneous intellectual arguments or phrasings. One day, a mother and a baby visited a group home where three young men with mental retardation lived. When they left, one of the young men, David, discovered they had left behind a small, inexpensive toy. David insisted that the toy be returned to the baby. Staff tried all kinds of arguments to persuade David that it wasn't that important, but David wouldn't budge from his position. David was, of course, correct, and the toy was returned.

15. Less resistance to a relationship with the divine, e.g. God, possibly due to fewer intellectual barriers to the process.

In discussing these gifts of people with mental retardation, Wolfensberger warns that there is always a danger when discussing a group of people. He didn't want to be looked at as overgeneralizing or stereotyping. He also pointed out that people might accuse him of portraying people with mental retardation as "holy innocents." It's a shame that we have to think about these concerns when discussing the gifts of people we care about. It is possible, however, that people will assume that these qualities automatically apply to all people with mental retardation or that they comprise the sum total of that person's personality. No downs, only ups; no problems, only pluses; no concerns or worries, only bliss. Of course, this isn't true. Parents often know better than anyone else that people with disabilities are multi-faceted human beings.

In addition to the gifts identified by Wolfensberger, which may or may not apply to your child, there are other gifts. For example, Howard Gardner, a researcher on the subject of creativity, reminds us that gifts come in many different forms. He says that special abilities can come in seven different areas:

1. Language - People who like to make up stories or just play around with words are often gifted with linguistic intelligence.

2. Math and Logic - This type of intelligence is evidenced by people who like to work with numbers or explore the relationships of different concepts. This type of intelligence is usually measured on a standard intelligence test given in schools.

3. Spatial Reasoning - This is the ability to imagine how things or shapes will look in space or to understand how objects can fit together. Builders, mechanics, people who like puzzles, kids who play well with blocks are all examples of people who are exercising their spatial reasoning.

4. Movement/kinetic - Dancers, athletes, crafters (like whittlers) are gifted with the ability to reason with their bodies. These people use their bodies to solve problems or accomplish tasks.

5. Music - People gifted with musical intelligence are attracted to sounds, either by making sounds with their voice or hands or using instruments.

6. Interpersonal - This is the type of reasoning we use to get along with other people. Natural born leadership, the ability to motivate others, and empathy are all forms of interpersonal intelligence.

7. Intrapersonal - This is the ability to know yourself. This may be the most difficult type of intelligence to identify because it is often hidden. Someone who understands their abilities and their tolerance for frustration may be an example of someone gifted with intrapersonal intelligence.

It's important to recognize that the testing system which labeled your child is very limited. It probably only looked at language, math, and logic. Even then, there is much room for error. For example, there have been some very gifted story tellers who would do very poorly on I.Q. tests. I believe every person is gifted in some way. I find Gardner's idea of multiple intelligences to be very liberating when considering the gifts of people with cognitive disabilities. I have met people who scored poorly on intelligence tests but could sing any song they had ever heard, plan and maintain a beautiful garden, or fix any small mechanical device you put before them. The concept that all people have some kind of gift, despite their educational record, seems to be getting more and more popular, with books such as *Wishcraft* by Barbara Sher and

Born to Fly: How to Discover and Encourage Your Child's Natural Talent by Thom Black leading the way.

We don't do a very good job of helping people identify and nurture their gifts in this society. How many of us, when complimented, respond by pointing out some negative aspect of our accomplishment? As a rule, people spend much more time thinking about their flaws than they do about their strengths. The problem is magnified when discussing people with disabilities.

I attended a training session on people with disabilities some time ago with a lot of eagerness. One of the speakers was going to talk about relationships and the gifts people with disabilities bring to those relationships. I sat among a couple of hundred people, pen poised, ready to hear something human service workers almost never talk about. The speaker got up and talked about some guy's smile. I felt cheated. Couldn't she do better than that? Not that a nice smile isn't a good thing, but I refuse to believe that's all there is to this person. I have since noticed that you frequently hear trite things like this when discussing the gifts of people with cognitive disabilities.

> *"He's very trusting."*
> *"She allowed us to exercise our gifts of charity because she was so needy."*
> *"He had a great smile."*

I feel that these descriptions are too limited. Hearing comments like this makes me feel that someone didn't spend enough time really exploring what the person with the disability has to offer. Some of these are great qualities, particularly if you are musing upon what is wrong with society today, but that can't be all there is to a person. What about:

> *"He loves to cook. He's always looking in magazines for new recipes to try."*
> *"She's really got a green thumb. Plants really respond to her. She can grow anything."*
> *"He is religious about getting committee work done. If two weeks go by and we haven't talked, he's on the phone asking about our next meeting."*

IDENTIFYING YOUR CHILD'S GIFTS

When you first try to pinpoint your child's gifts, you may run up against several common roadblocks. First, as mentioned previously, you may be more used to seeing your child's weaknesses than his strengths, after years of working with professionals who look at people with disabilities in terms of their deficiencies. Second, you may have trouble identifying your child's gifts because of his lack of exposure to the world. Wolfensberger calls this "impoverishment of experience," meaning that people with disabilities often do not have the same types of experiences that typical people have. Consequently, they may not have had an opportunity to find their special niche or talent yet. The job then becomes one of exposing your child to as many different opportunities as possible and then supporting and nurturing those that he is attracted to. (See "Expanding Relationships" later in this chapter for more information.) Third, you may need to broaden your view of what a "strength" is. Many people, especially human service workers, have a very narrow view of strengths. While strengths *can* be measured in terms of how many puzzles you can complete and the number of words you speak, it can also be a strong interest or a wonderful personality trait. Does your son love music, even if he can't sing? That's a strength, a way to make a connection to other people. Is he really funny? Into videos? A hard worker once he knows what to do? Tenacious? The possibilities are endless.

Gardner's list of different intelligences may give you some ideas of where to start in investigating your child's strengths. For example, if your son enjoys singing, you may want to think of him as having high musical intelligence and look for musical activities that will help him develop his ability. You could get symphony tickets, look for a job in a record store, and investigate joining the church choir. If your son enjoys putting together puzzles, that's spatial intelligence at work. You may want to consider exposing him to model building, repairing simple things, or working on a construction site. Use Gardner's list to expand your thinking about things your child may enjoy and do well.

You may want to ask objective observers what they perceive your child's strengths to be. You could talk with a teacher, a speech therapist, or a coach about what they like about your child. Ask other parents too. As a starter, you may want to simply ask these people, "why do you like my son?" Their answers will give you clues to his strengths. Also ask family members, including your other children, to help you remember things that your child enjoys doing and what he seems to do well.

If you are still stuck, you may want to have an aptitude survey done by a psychologist to determine what strengths your child may have. There are even some tests that use pictures to help identify the gifts of people who can't speak. Possible options include the Geist Picture Interest Inventory, Revised, published by Western Psychological Services in Los Angeles; the Reading Free Vocational Interest Inventory, Revised, published by Elbern Publications; the Social and Prevocational Information Battery (SPIB), published by CTB/McGraw Hill; and the Non-Reading Aptitude Battery of the United States Employment Service, published by the U.S. Department of Labor. These tests usually involve having a trained tester show a series of pictures and asking questions designed to determine the individual's interests and abilities. Different tests are appropriate for different ability levels, so it is important to make sure that the one being used is right for your son or daughter. I'm sure that there are other aptitude surveys available; ask a local psychologist for guidance.

THE MYTH OF COMMUNITY READINESS

Sometimes parents worry that their child may not have the skills necessary to get involved with some kind of community activity. It is a myth, however, that people need a certain level of skills to join the community. Present thinking in the human service field is that everyone, no matter what their disability, can live in the community. Professionals are finding that the best way to obtain such skills is actually within the setting itself, not in some simulated or phony setting. People with cognitive disabilities often have trouble adapting things they learn in a special program to events in the real world, so it's now considered best to offer them support while learning in the real world, bypassing all the readiness training.

There's a saying in the field of cognitive disabilities that "`pre' means never," meaning that "pre-vocational" or "pre-socialization" may actually keep you from working or socializing successfully. There is an increasing feeling that such programs simply waste time with no measurable gain for the person receiving the training. It can be embarrassing to take someone with poor social skills out and about, and you may need professional assistance to do it, but if you really want your child to learn to deal with the real world, "in vivo" is the only way.

INVOLVING YOUR CHILD

Before you actually begin expanding your child's social contacts, you need to sit down with your child and carefully explain the process. Even if your child is non-verbal, take the time to explain what is happening. Depending upon your child's personality, you may need to explain the benefits of meeting new people. Emphasize how much fun it can be to get to know new people and to share an interest with someone. Be careful to ensure that your child doesn't feel as if you're dumping him. Reassure him that you love him. Most people with disabilities like to meet new people and will take all this in stride. Some may find it more difficult. You know your child best. Try to determine what his concerns are, if any, and follow your instincts in reassuring him. You'll find that it helps to clarify the process in your own mind, as well as showing your child that his feelings are important. Try to arouse your child's enthusiasm by getting his ideas on new activities to try.

Some people with cognitive disabilities will say "yes" to any new activity just to be agreeable. Most will give you a true idea of their preferences. If your child happens to be one of the "agreeable" types, suggest several activities and encourage him to pick one or two. If your child has difficulty understanding speech, use pictures from magazines to show him different activities. If you get no response at all, just try something, based on your best guess about what your child may enjoy. If it doesn't work out, drop out of the activity and try something else.

Build on your child's current interests. Look at how he likes to spend his time, and use Gardner's list to expand your thinking about other possibilities. In some cases, you will need to deal with simple fear of the unknown. Your child may have to overcome years of isolation or a strong attachment to you or your spouse. In these situations, it's best to start gradually and with a lot of support and encouragement. Building new relationships can be a scary thing, so proceed gently.

INVOLVING OTHERS

You will also want to secure the support of your spouse and family, if you have any. A spouse or other family member can help you pinpoint your child's interests and strengths, add to your network of contacts, and provide moral support when things don't go as planned. If your spouse is not supportive at this point, you may want to try having her read this book. If your partner doesn't see why others may want to spend time with your child, go through the process of identifying gifts and talents together. If your spouse emphasizes finances as a means to a secure future, talk about some of the problems with strict trust guidelines. (As Chapter 10 explains, these include inflexibility, vulnerability to changing laws, the dynamic nature of your child's life, etc.). Support your spouse, though, in setting up something that will allow some flexibility in the future. You may also want to include your spouse in planning some activities or identifying possible contacts.

Sometimes, involvement is a key to cooperation. It's important to recognize that a highly resistant spouse may be reacting to years of messages that people with cognitive disabilities need to be segregated with their "own kind." For years, parents were told by professionals that this was the best thing to do for their children. It can be hard to suddenly see things differently, especially if you bought into those messages and decided to "send your child away." Admitting that your child needs a lot of community contacts may mean that you didn't make the best decision years ago. This is a hard thing to accept. Emphasize that you were acting on the best expert advice available at the time and that more is being learned every day about people with cognitive disabilities. Now, research has proven that anyone can live successfully in the community when provided with appropriate supports. And, for several reasons, people are better off having as many contacts as possible.

EXPANDING RELATIONSHIPS

Now, armed with the results of conversations with your child about activities that he might like to try and your own uncanny understanding of your child and what he might be good at, you're ready to look for ways to hook up some relationships.

There are two basic ways of expanding numbers of relationships: 1) you can join a group and meet people, or 2) you can ask people you already know to introduce you to others.

Joining a Group

We'll look at the more public approach of joining groups first. First, let's look at some ideas for introducing people with disabilities to others in the community. These ideas are drawn from two booklets written by Mary O'Connell, a research writer for the Center for Urban Affairs and Policy Research, Northwestern University ("Getting Connected: How to Find Out about Groups and Organizations in Your Neighborhood" and "The Gift of Hospitality: Opening the Doors of Community Life to People with Disabilities." O'Connell wrote of methods that The Community Life Project used to identify as many groups as possible in an older Chicago neighborhood. The methods can be used by anyone in any community, often yielding surprising results.

1. Using newspapers, directories, and other printed sources. The Project reviewed weekly community newspapers and listed any mention of events, clubs, meetings, sports and recreational groups that people could join. They also reviewed the nearest city's paper for similar information, focusing on the Sunday edition. Local magazines often run listings of volunteer opportunities and self-help groups. The project also suggested reviewing special purpose newspapers which may be published by churches, political parties, environmental groups, etc.

A lot of times there is some kind of directory already published by somebody—the newspaper, the United Way, the library which lists community organizations. These may be a little out of date, but don't let that stop you. Even if Jane Doe isn't the president of the Horticultural Society anymore, she can probably tell you who is and when the group meets.

Broader, more general directories exist which can be used to ferret out information on your area. O'Connell mentions three—the phone book (looking under associations and organizations and fraternities); the *Encyclopedia of Associations*, often available in public libraries; and self-help directories, frequently published by hospitals. Sometimes these guides only list national organizations. If you want to find local or state chapters of a particular group, call the national organization and ask for the chapter closest to you. They are usually happy to help you get in touch.

2. Contacting local institutions. If you find that a lot of groups meet at the local community center, call up the community center and ask for information on all the different groups that meet there. Also ask if they know of any groups that share a specific interest of your child's, such as gardening or painting. Other possible sources of information include libraries, parks, recreational programs, and churches. The Community Life Project feels that religious organizations are very important to identifying community associations. They recommend getting started by obtaining a list of churches from hotels, hospitals, or the phone book and then asking the church which groups it sponsors and who uses the church as a meeting place.

3. Contacting individuals. The project spent a good bit of time asking individuals in a specific geographical area to identify the groups that they participate in or knew of. Parents can do the same thing by asking their neighbors, local merchants, etc. about groups in which they participate. Parents can ask similar questions to those asked by the project:

- ✐ Can you name any groups you've heard of or participated in? Does it meet in your neighborhood?
- ✐ Is there a local neighborhood organization in your area? What about a block club?
- ✐ Is there any church or religious organization you're involved with?
- ✐ If yes, within the church, are there any other groups or clubs that you're a part of?
- ✐ Are there any other special interest groups that you or people in your family are in—such as women's or men's groups, veteran's organizations, artistic clubs, or other clubs?
- ✐ Are there any things you do for relaxation or recreation in the area?
- ✐ What about informal groups? Do you get together or associate with your neighbors?
- ✐ How else do you feel a part of the community? How else do you get involved in your neighborhood?

One other source that I think deserves to be mentioned is your local government. People who work in government are usually very well connected and know a lot about your community. The local township or county secretary, the county commissioner, the state representative's office staff, are all probably good people to tap for ideas and suggestions. Parents could simply call up and ask if there is a list of recreational activities or clubs for the area. Again, if your child has a specific interest, you can ask about a related club.

There are also many times a whole host of advisory councils or committees who come together to look into improving the area sponsored by the government. For example, close to my home in Washington Township, a community of 3200 people, the government has eight different citizen advisory committees which do all kinds of things like work on recycling projects and promote the local community park. To get a list of councils or committees, call the mayor's office, or the county commissioners, and explain that you want a list of groups that use volunteers to advise the borough, or the county. Ask them to refer you to the appropriate person. Many times, these groups are crying out for volunteers and will be happy to help you get involved. You can also ask for assistance from a related non-profit agency or your local library.

Of course, your work will be lessened somewhat if you already have an idea of your child's gifts as we suggested in the beginning of the chapter. If she really loves music, you'll want to look into arts organizations. I wouldn't discount other groups however. Maybe she could just as easily fit in at the local library where they play Vivaldi over lunch.

O'Connell has three other suggestions for bringing people with disabilities into contact with other people. Other than joining groups, she emphasizes that you can start just about anywhere:

Patronize small businesses. Get a haircut at the neighborhood beauty parlor, eat lunch every day at the same diner or volunteer at the local day care center. These places often have a cluster of regular customers or a shop owner who is friendly and outgoing. They are often "in the know" and can suggest other opportunities for making friends.

Churches. Joining a local religious community can be a real boon for people with disabilities. Churches and synagogues are often looking for all kinds of assistance, from chaperoning youth trips to making baked goods to helping out with caring for their grounds. In addition, many congregations welcome people with disabilities and would be interested in helping them resolve problems such as a need for housing, dealing with illness, or grieving for a loved one.

Public places. O'Connell suggests that places like the public library, police station, and civil defense office may hold opportunities for people with disabilities to volunteer or meet other people. In our community, we have a public swimming pool where you can find all sorts of people on any given afternoon between Memorial Day and Labor Day.

Bring the Community to You

Another idea for meeting new people comes from New Hats, Inc., a nonprofit agency from Salt Lake City, Utah, which specializes in providing supports for people with disabilities. New Hats suggests organizing

some community or neighborhood activities yourself. Ideas included in
their booklet "Using Natural Supports in Community Integration" are:

- Neighborhood yard sale, spring cleanup, dump runs
- Fix up a house or yard; trade skills
- Create a community center, a playground, community recreation program, thrift store, flea market, community talk radio
- Create (or join) groups/clubs: hiking, biking, photography, book reading, horse riding, boating, sewing, pet or animal training, pottery making
- Share the cost and use of land, a vacation home, condominium, RV
- Share catalogs and order things together: vitamins, sale catalog items, bulk foods, etc.
- Two households share cost and use of items: vacuum, bicycles, camping equipment, tools, VCR machine and tapes
- Create a slide show (or a series) with individuals contributing slides from their own collections
- Invite people over for: pancake breakfasts, games like Pictionary or Charades, birthdays/celebrations/parties, open house, making Christmas cards or Valentines, Easter egg decorating/hunt
- Develop a lending library of books, tapes, records, videos
- Exchange skills of a craft or hobby
- Rent out things that you buy: bicycles, video machines, canners, juicers
- Do pot luck dinners, barbecues
- Make ice cream and have everybody bring ingredients for something to put on it
- Start (or join) a co-op: food, housing, child care, respite care, child-watch
- Share a garden or agricultural project
- Special projects: canning, food drying, making root beer/sasparilla, baking Christmas cookies, fix-up projects, quilt making

⊘ Traveling and trips: zoo, special places, aviary, concerts, movies, camping, outings

⊘ Share rides or become part of a car pool

⊘ Assist (or start) group efforts: community celebrations/festivals, fundraising events, disaster clean-up, dress up as Santa, adopt-a-highway, neighborhood crime prevention

⊘ Exchange services and skills with others: mentoring, apprenticeship, tutoring

Places to Go, Things to Do

New Hats, Inc. has also catalogued a sample list of community resources. Use this list to get ideas on what to do on a Saturday when you're tired of the same old thing or to find a fresh approach to solving a problem. Sometimes we develop habits, going to the same places over and over. Look over the following suggestions to add some new options for meeting people and expanding contacts.

RECREATION AND LEISURE

golf course	spectator sports	movie theater
video rental	novelty shop	bowling alley
parks	pools	volleyball
planetarium	riding stables	skating rinks
amusement parks	resorts	gyms
winter sports	multi-purpose centers	county recreation
YWCA/YMCA	game room or arcade	games
zoo	local, national & state parks	campsites
gardens	photography	museums
social circle	ice cream parlors	plays, concerts
television	water sports	art galleries
picnic areas	wilderness areas *(lakes, ponds, mountains, rivers, beaches, oceans, deserts, streams)*	

Routine/Community Life

These places may hold volunteer or work opportunities for your son or daughter.

library	grocery store	laundromats
fire station	post office	police station
buses, depots	train stations	airport
travel agencies	cabs	cars/carpools
bicycle shops or clubs	motorcycle clubs	city/county building

Shelter, Material Possessions

residential agencies	Social Services field offices
shoe store	malls
department stores	thrift shops
hardware stores	convenience stores
laundromats	motels, hotels

Work/Money

sheltered employment	community based employment
banks	Social Security office
Medicare/Medicaid Office	community centers
job service	Department of Labor
credit union	financial advisors
vocational rehabilitation office	

Physical/Biological

restaurants, coffee shops	Meals on Wheels
Food Stamps	community cafeteria
dental office	doctor's office
medical offices	chiropractor
barber, beauty shops	American Red Cross
special equipment retailers	occupational therapy
physical therapy	clinics
hospitals	alternative health care providers
spas	yoga
aerobics	weight training
counselor, therapist	drug/alcohol/substance abuse rehab

SPIRITUALITY/SERVICE

church

nature

news: TV and radio

music

volunteer organizations

newspapers, books, magazines

PERSONAL RIGHTS

legal center

legal center for the handicapped

Governor's Committee on Employment for the Handicapped

lawyer/attorney

mental health center

Planned Parenthood

hospice

Association for Retarded Citizens (The Arc)

Mental Retardation Associations

Social Services

Council for Developmentally Disabled & Handicapped Persons

Legislative Coalition

Police

Vocational Rehabilitation Services

consumer groups

professional associations

RELATIONSHIPS: FRIENDS, FAMILY, SOCIAL LIFE

dances

Big Brother/Sister

relatives

see also Recreation/Leisure

see also Work

parties

clubs

child care agencies

dates

neighbors

counseling center

MENTAL STIMULATION

talking books

continuing education

community college or
    university

see also Recreation/Leisure

see also Work

evening classes

personal interests

hobbies

respite care

Zeroing In on an Activity

If you find that your child has many interests and you need to narrow your choices a bit, you can use the checklist below to assess possible places to start. This checklist will help you think about the type of environment in which your child is most likely to be successful.

Don't allow the checklist to narrow your thinking too much; don't let it be an excuse to be idle. For example, if your daughter likes to paint and uses a wheelchair and none of the possibilities for art classes are accessible, work with the most likely prospect on accommodating your daughter. Don't just give up.

ENVIRONMENTAL ISSUES CHECKLIST

❑ **Consider whether group members are likely to have the time and inclination to make new friends:**
- ✐ **Likely prospects** for friends might include people who are friendly, respected, outgoing, and involved in the activity for fun, to fill some spare time, or to make the world a better place.
- ✐ **Unlikely prospects** for friends might include people who are obsessed with winning or being the best at that particular activity (e.g., they want to be the soccer champions), or harried businesspeople who are involved in the activity because their job requires it. Be careful, though about dismissing anyone prematurely.

❑ **Have other people with disabilities previously been involved in the activity?** This may be a sign that members welcome the participation of people with disabilities.

❑ **Think about where meetings/activities are held:**
- ✐ Could your child reach the meeting place on his own (e.g., by bus) if he wanted to?

Expand Your Child's Current Network

So far, we've been focusing on the more public approach to increasing exposure to new people: identify an interest, talent, or capacity and join a group, formal or informal. O'Connell reminds us that another option is to tap into and try to broaden any existing relationships your child may have. Is there someone your child already knows who may be willing to introduce him to new groups of people?

    ✐ If your child is in a wheelchair, are the facilities physically accessible?

    ✐ If your child has difficulty sitting still for long periods of time, is there enough room for him to wander around?

    ✐ Is there anything in the setting that is likely to distract or bother your child (like humming fluorescent lights, high noise level?) Other issues?

❑ **Are there dues or other costs involved in participation?** Can your child afford them?

❑ **Consider how much structure your child needs.** Will this activity likely provide him with too much or too little?

❑ **Consider your child's past experiences and behavior.** If he's very shy or has significant problems with behavior, you might want to try small group or one-on-one activities. If your child just seems to lack confidence, can you audit the activity or class, visit the site before signing up, or get some private lessons?

If the answer is "no," your child is in good company. As we have already discussed, people with disabilities often lead sheltered, secluded lives. If they meet people, it's usually other people with disabilities. There are many reasons for this, including the impression that the general public sometimes has of people with disabilities, or the encouragement of family members who just think that this is the way people with disabilities are supposed to live.

The social service system, too, often discourages people with disabilities from nurturing their existing relationships. For example, when someone moves into a group home, the provider agency will often tell parents that their visits upset the person, or that they can only visit once a month, etc. Parents get the message that their involvement is not welcome, and they gradually eliminate their contact with their child. Other times, people who live in residential programs are simply not assisted in getting together with people they may have met, due to staffing problems or a lack of transportation, etc. Sometimes this encouragement to cut off outside relationships is intentional, and sometimes it's done in the interest of protecting people. Whatever the purpose, many people who live in residential programs lead extremely isolated lives. Many times, people who live at home with their families have more relationships with non-paid, nondisabled people than those who live in institutions or community programs.

Segregated Activities

When choosing activities to get involved in, you may want to avoid those that cater to groups of people with disabilities. Even though these may occur in a public setting or be run by a non-disability-related community organization, such activities perpetuate the idea that people with disabilities are "special" and very different from the rest of us. It's often harder for people to understand and approach people with disabilities if they are all lumped together in a group. This tends to promote the idea that "they are better off with their own kind."

If your child takes part mostly in segregated activities, don't lose heart. Many times there are opportunities to broaden a person's contacts even when participating in disability-focused programs.

Does your child go swimming with a group of people with disabilities? How about taking your child to the pool when it's open to the general public? Or better yet, how about joining the swimming team for nondisabled people? Does your child participate in a segregated horseback riding therapy program? How about going to a horse show or volunteering for a show committee? Is your son in a horticultural therapy program? How about a job at a local greenhouse, or taking a class on gardening at the local community college?

George used to attend a self-contained classroom. His mother was upset because his three sisters who were not disabled went off to school each day with their friends on the school bus, while George waited for the Special Education Program van. Her daughters were invited to neighborhood birthday parties and sleep-overs, but George's classmates lived so far away that they never got together to play. George's mother felt bad for George; he really liked other kids but because he wasn't in school with them, no one in the neighborhood seemed to know who he was. George's mom fought the recommendation of special education personnel and won a place for him in a typical classroom, in the same school he would attend if he didn't have a disability. He has an aide who adapts the classroom activities so that he can participate. He's learned to speak a lot better and kids in the neighborhood say hi to him at McDonald's. The other week, he got his first invitation to a neighborhood pool party. George's mother is delighted. She says, "these neighbor kids are going to grow up and be legislators and businessmen. Maybe one of them will give him a job someday."

❖

Joe used to live at a private institution for people with mental retardation. When he turned 21, his dad decided that he was ready to move into his own apartment and get a job. Together, they found a job

*in the mail room of a nearby corporation. Joe
decided to throw himself a party for his 25th birthday and invited several people he had met since
moving out of the institution. When his dad arrived
at the party, he was surprised to see about 50
people crammed into the small apartment. Circulat-
ing throughout the room, he met a doctor, a corporate vice-president, and a bus driver. Everyone was
having a good time, thanks in part to the food and
drinks Joe had arranged on a buffet. Joe's father
was astounded. "I never thought all these people
would come," he said. "Joe is really popular."*

Your new network may result in more than friendships. It's
likely that your child's opportunities for fun will increase and, if
you talk about the need, employment opportunities may arise.
One parent I know networked her child with students who attended a nearby college. She simply went into the college placement office and asked for names of students who might be interested in meeting her son. One relationship went so well that she
asked if the young man would like to share a condominium with
her son. He accepted and now swaps assistance with her son's
daily living activities like banking and cooking for rent.

Professional "Matchmakers"

Some groups exist just to match people up. I wouldn't rule these
out. Big Brothers/Big Sisters will often match people with disabilities with an older nondisabled person. Singles groups are another possibility for the adult with disabilities. Some communities have "friend" or "citizen" advocacy programs which concentrate on matching people with disabilities with well-liked individuals in the same geographic area. For more information on Citizen or Friend Advocacy programs, see Chapter 12.

Person Centered Planning

Person Centered Planning processes look at a person's future with
the support of a small group of people committed to the person

with the disability. The purpose of these processes is to formulate a plan that will determine the person's goals and wishes and the kind of support necessary to achieve them. In some states, person centered planning has taken the place of, or augmented, traditional Individualized Habilitation Plans (IHP). The IHP is often required by regulations and governs the type of services people receive in day and residential programs. Person centered plans are thought to be an improvement on the "cookie cutter" approach of the more traditional IHP.

One person centered planning process, Personal Futures Planning, developed by Beth Mount, looks at the person's background, positive and negative experiences, preferences, immediate and long-term goals, and relationships. A person centered planning process can help clarify the roles of friends and the support they may be able to provide to the person. Also, if it's decided that the person wants to expand his social network, the planning group can act as resources, helping to introduce the person to new opportunities for friendship.

If you haven't had the opportunity to do so, you may want to look into having a facilitator conduct a person centered planning process focusing on your child. This is usually done for adults who have already graduated from the school system, but you can certainly request the service for your minor child. Contact your state office of human services for assistance in finding someone skilled in facilitating person centered planning in your area. Sometimes, the government may provide this service for you; other times you will have to pay for it yourself.

You may be wondering how person centered planning processes differ from the methods described in this book. A major difference is that this book is more narrowly focused. This book outlines ways that you can build your child's personal network and how you can encourage those friends to advocate for your child after your death. In contrast, person centered planning processes are all encompassing and are usually concerned with what's happening right now. They may indeed note that your child needs more relationships, but they will also talk about his need to learn to cook, to get a new roommate, or to identify appropriate service providers. The process described in this book assists parents in recruiting non-paid advocates who can help their child through person centered planning processes in years to come. The processes are not mutually exclusive; rather, this book's focus on relationships can help make a successful person centered plan.

Real Work

Another social service option which could result in opportunities for new relationships is through employment. There are many opportunities for new relationships in both competitive and supported employment. (In supported employment, a person, typically with severe disabilities, works at a real job—something that a nondisabled person might do—with on-going support of a job coach). If your child is already employed, explore the work place for new relationships. If the typical "let's get together after work" invitation doesn't seem feasible, try to organize car pooling or ask about having one of the other employees mentor for your son or daughter. Mentoring can involve helping your child meet people, resolve work conflicts, explain company memos, etc.

Some work places have informal opportunities for employees to get together off duty, like company softball teams. At my sister's place of employment, most of the women meet on Saturday mornings and go to Weight Watchers. It would be relatively easy to sign up your daughter and review the information with her. This would give her something to talk to her co-workers about during the week, deepening their relationship.

LIVING AWAY FROM HOME

If your child lives away from home, on his own or in some kind of staffed residential program, you may not start out knowing as much about his neighborhood as you do your own. However, if you apply Mary O'Connell's suggestions for "getting connected," you should be able to come up with several opportunities that you and your child can agree on very quickly. If your child needs assistance in meeting new people, you will want to introduce your child to his new options yourself, if at all possible. If this isn't possible, you will need to help work out transportation and in many cases, rely on residential program staff. This can be tough, but is rarely impossible. If you can't get the staff to freely agree to work on introducing your child to new options, you may want to negotiate a minimum number of contacts or specific activities through the annual program planning process. For example, add to your child's plan, "John will participate in choir and cooking classes at the community college at least weekly." This should help get the ball rolling.

THE WORK OF A LIFETIME

Try not to look at developing new relationships as a once-and-done thing. Look for people who have the ability to open doors for your child, and encourage as many people as possible to join in your child's life. Expanding and modifying your child's social contacts is the work of a lifetime. You need to focus on people who can open doors to other people who can open doors, and so on. You also need to recognize that meeting people is just the beginning. Developing and nurturing relationships takes months, even years. Unless someone has a strong commitment to your child, it is unlikely that he or she will be willing to look out for him for the long term. Strong commitments take time to develop. At this point, you probably need some suggestions on how to actually introduce your child to others and how to encourage a relationship. Many ideas for getting people together are discussed later, in Chapter 7.

CHAPTER 5

WHAT ABOUT THE YOUNGER CHILD WITH DISABILITIES?

"My child has developmental disabilities, but she's only five years old. My husband and I are young too. We don't have to worry about any of this now, do we? When should we start to plan?"

Hold everything. You need to plan for your child's future now, no matter what her age. Many parents mistakenly think that they can wait until they're a lot older before they have to worry about what will happen to their child after they die. You could die at any time. Parents should always put a will together. (For more information on wills, see Chapter 10.) And, if your goal is to see your child surrounded by a group of caring, supportive people after your death, you need to network her early. Furthermore, the earlier you start this process of networking your child, the easier it will be.

Expectations today are simply different for people with disabilities than they were twenty years ago. Parents of young children say that they want their child to be part of the community, and they won't settle for anything less. Sheltered workshops and group homes might be okay for other people, they say, but I want my child to have more. Jobs and home ownership are now the goals for the new generation of people with disabilities.

Fortunately, society is actively figuring out how to serve people with disabilities in more typical community places and in more normal ways. Minor children in particular have a lot of advantages today—not the least of which is the trend to include them with nondisabled children in public schools. The Americans with Disabilities Act (ADA) also has opened up a lot of options to people with disabilities, such as typical camps and community centers. This federal law prohibits discrimination against individuals with disabilities by most facilities open to the general public, and also prohibits certain types of job discrimination. The ADA has not yet generated a great deal of case law; that is, there have not been that many court cases challenging specific types of discrimination. The law does, however provide tremendous opportunities for people with cognitive disabilities to gain access to typical recreational programs and other public facilities.

For adults with disabilities, the trend is toward more community-integrated, less restrictive settings. In twenty more years, group homes may be very small and sheltered workshops may be on their way out. (Sheltered workshops are programs in which adults with disabilities learn vocational skills and may be paid to do some job tasks, but are segregated from nondisabled workers.) Instead, almost everyone may have some kind of vocational training program within typical employment or recreational settings.

Researchers say that inclusion in schools benefits both disabled and nondisabled students tremendously. Students with disabilities show an improvement in social skills and adaptive behavior; students without disabilities show a stronger appreciation for

diverse gifts and talents. Many supporters of inclusion in education feel that it holds the key for successful reformation of the
entire education system.

Some are dubious of this trend to provide services in natural
settings. They say that it's a form of dumping people without providing enough support. And it *is* true that some government officials believe that using generic community services, such as neighborhood playground programs for typical kids or the local senior
citizen program, is simply cheaper than setting up large, specialized campus-style institutions. Parent advocates need to be ever
vigilant, and make sure that in the process of obtaining fewer re-
strictions in their lifestyles, people with disabilities are not also
provided with less support than they need.

One positive outcome of the trend toward providing
supports in the least restrictive environment is that people with
disabilities more naturally come in contact with more nondisabled people.

INCLUSION

*"I had a friend who had her child mainstreamed about
ten years ago. Talk about dumping! That kid was just
dumped into a couple of regular education classes, then
taken back to his special ed class for the rest of the day.
He didn't do well, academically or socially. His mom said
it was the worst decision they ever made. Now they're
talking about inclusion for my daughter, Samantha. I
don't want her dumped like that other kid."*

There's a lot of confusion about the difference between the terms
"mainstreaming" and "inclusion." I like to think of inclusion as an
evolution of mainstreaming. It's true that a few years ago, the
education field experimented with placing selected kids with special needs in typical classrooms for part of the day. The special-
needs child had to "earn" her opportunity to prove herself in the
"mainstream" of school life. The child had to demonstrate an ability to keep pace with the teacher and the rest of the class. Very

little was done to modify the class for the child. The child was expected to sink or swim along with the regular education kids, for a few carefully chosen subjects. Sometimes, the child did okay. A lot of times, the kid sank.

Educators and parents learned a lot from those experiences. Today, inclusion means that there is a commitment to educate each and every child in their home school—the school they would attend if they had no disability. It involves bringing supports into the classroom to help the child benefit from the class. Supports can be special assistive technology, personal aides, modifications in curriculum, etc. Inclusion has more of a philosophical basis than mainstreaming. Proponents of inclusion believe that good schools get better when they include all the children in the school's neighborhood. In fact, many people believe that within the inclusion effort lies the key to successful educational reform. Inclusion is being encouraged by such organizations as the National Association of State Boards of Education (NASBE). NASBE's publication, *Winning Ways*, a guide to implementing inclusion in public schools, emphasizes that it was intended to help "all students across the country who will benefit from an education that is based on their individual needs rather than where they fit in the system."

Dumping a kid with special needs into a regular classroom is not inclusion. Don't let anyone tell you that it is. Advocate for the supports that your child will need to make her educational experience a success.

> *"I think this whole inclusion thing is just another attempt to cut services to people with disabilities. It's just another social service fad. I really don't see why I should subject my child to a regular education class. What could they possibly provide that she can't get in her special school?"*

Most parents are extremely good advocates for their children with disabilities. You know your child best. You know what she needs and what she doesn't need. You also owe it to your child to be as informed as possible about inclusion.

Parent Education and Assistance for Kids (PEAK), located in Colorado Springs, Colorado, is a national resource program for information on inclusion. PEAK cites nine different studies that show the following benefits to thoughtfully integrated children with disabilities:

- New genuine friendships develop between disabled and nondisabled friends.
- Integration efforts which include planned, sustained interactions between disabled and nondisabled peers show improved attitudes and interaction patterns.
- An increased number of IEP goals are met by students with disabilities in integrated settings.
- Students with disabilities are more motivated in learning activities with nondisabled friends.
- Regular education provides access to peer models to facilitate learning and appropriate behaviors.
- Through integration, students with disabilities encounter the expectations and diversity of our society.
- Graduates of integrated programs are more successful as adults.

PEAK also maintains that as a result of these benefits, traditional methods for providing special education are now being questioned. PEAK cites studies that found:

- Traditional services have been designed around removing, caretaking, and deviance, rather than normalizing.
- Labeling and pull-out for special education service can cause students to be stigmatized. This can further isolate the student and increase the student's negative attitudes about school and learning.

It seems pretty clear that inclusion is highly beneficial when approached in an individualized, thoughtful way. At a minimum, having your daughter included in a regular classroom will help her develop valuable contacts and skills which she can draw upon for a fuller, more productive life.

Making Inclusion Work

"The school wants to put my son, Jeremy, into a third grade class. He's the right age, but I'm worried about it. Kids aren't very nice sometimes, and I'm afraid they'll tease him. The school wants to give him an aide, but I think that would just make him stick out like a sore thumb. Won't it wreck his self-confidence to have other kids mock him all day long?"

Parents of all children are concerned for their well-being. When your child has a disability, you can be even more concerned than usual. The truth is that kids in integrated settings aren't teased or hurt any more than kids who are in segregated settings. It may surprise parents to know that teasing goes on between students in special schools, trainees in workshops, and residents of institutions. Happily though, teasing in integrated programs is usually not as bad as parents anticipate. The kid with disabilities can usually take it in stride, having the same range of reactions to teasing that typical kids do. In addition, there are often good, kind-hearted typical kids who can get their peers to halt the teasing of a student with disabilities.

Parents are also concerned that being assigned an instructional aide can make their child be seen as separate or different. The truth is that segregation makes children seem even more different. I remember going to middle school and occasionally seeing special education students from a "self contained" classroom traveling through the school. This happened pretty rarely. None of us knew who they were. We didn't know their names. I heard kids refer to these students in derogatory ways. No doubt some of that would have been reduced if we could have had some kind of contact with them, if we could have known them as human beings.

It might help ease your mind to set up a daily communication system with the teacher. A notebook that is passed back and forth, a simple checklist, or a weekly phone conversation can help you keep tabs on what is happening during the school day. It's important not to assume that your son will automatically be accepted by the other classmates. Sometimes, inclusion is done thoughtlessly and without adequate supports. The student with the disability for example, may have to sit at a different table at lunch, with his aide instead of the other students. Be on the alert for problems like this. Address them with the aide and the teacher as they come up. While sitting in a regular classroom is almost always better than being in a segregated setting, you need to do what you can to help your son fit in with his new classmates as well.

> *"I want to have my daughter included in our local middle school, but the special education department isn't very supportive. They say they're doing inclusion with elementary school-aged kids but not with middle school children. They tell me she's just too immature and too far behind academically. I really want her to get to know local kids, and I think school is the best way to do this. Any suggestions?"*

First, try really hard to obtain the support of the school's administrator. Meet with the middle school principal, introduce your daughter, and try to educate him or her on inclusion. If you can win the support of the building administrator, you've won the war. Parents who have been through this often feel that the building administrator can make or break an inclusive program. Do what you can to get this person on your side.

You also need to address the issue through your child's Individualized Education Program (IEP). Make sure that the IEP specifies that your child needs to have contact with nondisabled children. If school officials remain unwilling to try inclusion, remember that the Individuals with Disabilities Education Act (IDEA) offers parents due process procedures for resolving grievances about their child's special education program. Grievances can concern most problems with the way their child's education program is being implemented, and can be taken all the way to court if necessary. Your special education department must provide you with information on your rights under IDEA. If they can't or won't, contact one of the national advocacy organizations listed in Appendix C, and ask them for assistance.

IDEA and Section 504 of the Rehabilitation Act of 1973 require that schools educate children in the least restrictive setting possible. Court decisions, such as Sacramento City Unified School District v. Holland and Oberti v. Board of Education of the Borough of Clementon School District, have resulted in students with significant disabilities being placed in typical classrooms with supports. If you feel strongly enough, there is legal precedent to support your cause if you have to go to court to obtain an inclusive program for your child. In addition, your school is probably receiving federal grants which could be jeopardized if they try to stonewall you.

A faster, easier way to fight for inclusion is to file a civil rights complaint with the local Human Rights Commission or Civil Rights Office. Look these government offices up in the phone book. They'll come out and investigate, letting you know if there is a civil rights violation involved in not including your child. You don't need an attorney to file a complaint, but you can certainly involve one if you want. Simply call the office and request their form for complaints.

Each state has a review process for the department of education, with staffs that investigate complaints about the implementation of special education services. Call your state department of education to find out how to file a complaint in your area. Ask for the Office of Compliance or just explain that you have a complaint about special education services and you will most likely be pointed in the right direction.

It is true that most of the work on including students has been targeted at the elementary school level. However, there are resources that can help you get the information you need to implement an inclusive program for an older child. Your state department of education will, in all likelihood, have experts who can assist your school in making inclusion work; likewise universities and colleges with strong education and special education programs. PEAK, as well as other parent education training centers throughout the country, offers advice and consultation to parents all over the United States on how to integrate students with special needs into neighborhood schools.

"I fought hard for two years to have my daughter, Laura, included in her neighborhood school. She was all set to attend third grade this September. In July, the third grade teacher told me that the parents of her other kids were very upset that Laura would be in the same classroom as their children. The teacher said they were campaigning with the principal to have Laura removed. I can't believe it. Laura's so sweet; this is so unfair. Now I'm wondering if I did the wrong thing."

It sounds as if the teacher has concerns about Laura's participation and has shared those concerns with other parents. Think about it. I'm never told who's going to be in my kid's class until the class rosters are advertised in August. To make this a good year for everyone concerned, you can address the situation on several different levels.

First, the teacher. Many teachers don't support inclusion because they feel that they are being given more work. They feel they are already stretched to their limit by large classes of typical children; throw a kid with special needs into the mix and the teacher feels the situation is impossible. It's important to make sure that Laura has the support she needs to benefit from the class. Is an aide needed? Will there be a special education teacher available to both Laura and the classroom teacher? Talk with the teacher and try to determine what she thinks is needed for Laura to be included in third grade.

Some parents who have faced this situation have sent letters to each of the other students' families introducing their child and explaining why inclusion is important. Some have asked to meet with the other families. Most have found that once the families get to know someone like Laura, their concerns evaporate.

Other families of kids with disabilities have opted for a stronger approach. They file civil rights complaints as discussed above. What if you were discussing a child of a different race, they reason. A child with a disability shouldn't be treated any differently than any other minority.

You may indeed find that you are facing simple prejudice. Some parents decide not to fight these situations, pulling their child out of schools if they don't seem welcoming. You need to decide what's best for you and your child, weighing your strength and resources. Parents who fight for inclusion see it as a pathmaking role. They know that there will be other children coming who will want to be included in that classroom. They gather strength from the knowledge that those children will have an easier time because of their efforts. Such parents also feel that including children with disabilities in regular education classrooms now will ultimately result in a better life for their sons and daughters. Their classmates are the corporate presidents, legislators, and attorneys of tomorrow. Coming into contact with people with disabilities at an early age will make for a more tolerant society with more opportunities for everyone, no matter what their strengths and needs.

> *"What about extracurricular activities? My other son is on the football team, and that's where he meets most of his friends. How can my son with mental retardation fit in?"*

Again, let your son's interests guide you with extracurricular activities. Does he like sports? Maybe he can get involved in the track or football team. If he can't make the varsity or junior varsity team, how about intramural sports? If none of that seems feasible, how about serving as water boy or equipment manager for the football, basketball, or other team? Go to the advisor for the activity he would enjoy and work out some way for him to be involved. At minimum, he could probably attend practice and just watch. No doubt someone will come up with an idea eventually.

If your child really likes music, but doesn't play an instrument well enough to participate, consider getting him private lessons to hone his skills. If that won't work, meet with the band director and ask for advice. A child with severe disabilities may be able to participate in the percussion section, as equipment manager, a stage hand for concerts, or a crooked line spotter for marching band. At minimum, the child could sit in the daily practices and just enjoy the music.

You will want to look outside of school for recreational activities as well. Consider activities for both typical kids and for kids

with disabilities. For example, Little League baseball has set up a
"Challenger Division" which supports the participation of kids with
disabilities in America's favorite pastime. Your child may be interested in joining the scout troup for typical kids, a segregated scouting program, or both. For more ideas on activities outside of school,
see Chapter Four.

> *"To be perfectly honest, I don't see why nondisabled kids
> should want a kid with a disability in their classroom.
> How can this possibly benefit anyone but my daughter? I
> think she has a right to a good education and
> nondisabled friends, but I don't know that I would feel
> this way if I didn't have a kid with special needs."*

Actually, classmates of students with disabilities do benefit from
the experience. When someone with special needs is included in a
general education classroom, the whole class has an opportunity
to grow. The May, 1993, *Research Bulletin* from the Center for
Evaluation, Development, and Research in Indiana states that:

- Classmates can develop a sense of responsibility
  and enhanced self-esteem from inclusive programs.
- Classmates' understanding of the range of human
  experience can be enhanced.
- Classmates can benefit from their disabled
  classmates as role models in coping with disabilities. As a result of advancements in medical
  services, most of those presently nondisabled
  children will survive to become persons with
  disabilities themselves one day.
- Classmates are enriched by the opportunity to
  have had friends with disabilities who successfully managed their affairs and enjoyed full lives.

As for the inevitable question about how including children
with disabilities will affect their classmates' test scores, studies
show that there is little to no impact. In fact, there is some data
that suggests that students who finish tests early and then help
their peers with disabilities may actually do better academically.

"My child's school won't provide her with a full-time aide. They say that very few children really need one and that they will provide other 'supplementary aids and services.' What else is there?"

Your school is right; not every included child comes with her own aide. Supplementary aids and services are determined on an individual basis and have to be specified in the IEP. Most often this is consultation and training for the regular education teacher, meaning that special education specialists would visit the regular education teacher periodically and give suggestions on how to improve communication skills, adapt curriculum, etc. Assistive technology is becoming more common, with some students using computers, speech synthesizers, FM amplification systems, braille typewriters, etc. Sometimes students are seated in a specific part of the class (the front row, away from the window, etc.) or have behavior management programs. Large print books are already pretty commonplace for students with visual impairments. Kids who have significant medical conditions may be accommodated by suctioning, positioning changes, blood sugar monitoring, or whatever.

By all means if your child needs an aide, request one. But don't assume that an aide is necessary in every situation. Sometimes aides may actually inhibit socialization between children. For instance, I have heard about a full-time classroom aide who sat with her student in a spot on the playground away from the other children. The other kids didn't feel they should approach their new classmate; the aide's presence seemed to be a signal to "stay away."

If you do get an aide, and your child needs assistance with things such as using the restroom, make sure someone is available throughout the day. I've also heard complaints about aides taking lunch breaks (which they deserve) and no one being available to assist the student with disabilities. This can result in an extremely embarrassing situation for everyone.

"My school is putting five kids with disabilities, including my son, into one third grade classroom. There will be twenty-five other kids in the class. Some of the other

*parents are unhappy about this, saying that they want
the kids with disabilities included in 'natural proportions.'
The teacher has a good reputation; she worked with a
child with autism last year and did well. She's even
frustrated. What's going on?"*

Sometimes a principal will try to assign all the kids with disabilities to one class for inclusion. Usually, there's a receptive teacher in that class who has a strong track record for including students with special needs. In addition, the principal may know that other teachers are not as receptive.

When inclusion proponents talk about natural proportions, they mean that people with disabilities should be included in numbers that statistically reflect the frequency in which they would normally appear. In your situation, it is unlikely that all those students would naturally be assigned to that classroom. The proportions are not typical. This can create a difficult working situation for the teacher, and in turn, a less than desirable environment for the students. The students with disabilities should be naturally distributed among the third grade classes, and all the teachers should accept responsibility for including them.

Inclusion can be an important mechanism for widening your child's network of friends. Many parents of kids with disabilities in inclusive education feel that they are creating a better world for their son or daughter. They say that the typical kids in the class will grow up to be doctors, legislators and restaurant owners, with a special sensitivity toward people with disabilities. This will help open doors when their children grow up and need jobs or government assistance.

During your child's school years, inclusion may help her become one of the gang. One mother I know switched her son from a segregated program to a typical school a few years ago. She was a little nervous about it; her son has Down syndrome and she was afraid he wouldn't fit in. A month after the switch, she called me and excitedly relayed that her son had been invited to a neighbor kid's birthday party for the first time. She felt strongly that this would not have happened if he had continued in the segregated program.

If you find that your child isn't making friends naturally, you can take steps to help the process along. Throw your kid a birthday party and invite all of her classmates. Put up an attractive swing set and make sure the neighbor kids feel welcome. Take a couple of kids with you when you go to the park. You can also solicit help from your child's teacher. The teacher can help identify likely candidates to be friends and work on fostering some friendships during the school day.

SHOULD MY CHILD HAVE ADULT FRIENDS?

"What about networking my younger child with adults? Should she get to know parents of other people with disabilities?"

I recommend a mix of adults and children as social contacts. Children are a natural choice because they often enjoy the same interests as your son or daughter. Adult friends are important too, because they can provide excellent role models and can expand your child's horizons. They can also be cultivated to serve as a guardian or trust officer in the event of your death.

Use naturally occurring opportunities to make sure that your child has several adults as well as children for friends. For example, make it a point for family members to spend time with her. If they take other children for visits, encourage them to take your child with a disability as well. Make sure the neighbors meet her. If you are so inclined, look into participating in some sort of church or religious activity. Make sure your own friends get to know her. Communicate to everyone that your child is an important part of your family. Your contacts will become her contacts.

Chances are that you personally will meet some good friends as you participate in advocacy efforts and parent groups. Parents of people with disabilities have a special camaraderie. A lot of them feel that they want to help make life better for people with disabilities, including through supporting other parents. By all means, if they are willing, make them part of your child's network. Just take care not to rely on only a few people. It can be tempting to just go to a parent support group, find a friendly, sympathetic parent, and feel as if you've networked your child sufficiently. It is certainly easier than approaching someone who may never have dealt with a person with a disability before. However, you do need to make a strong effort to meet other people too. The more diverse a group of people your child has surrounding her, the richer and more varied her opportunities will be. Your hard work will pay off.

CHAPTER 6

WHAT ABOUT BROTHERS
AND SISTERS?

B lood is thicker than water. There is a lot of truth
in that statement. Your children are likely to have
a relationship longer than any other relationship in their lives. Siblings often maintain a lifetime relationship with their brothers or
sisters despite marriage breakups, moves, changes in jobs, and ad-
ditions to responsibilities. When included in your child's network,
siblings can provide a continuity that you would be hard pressed
to find anywhere else in life today. A motivated sibling can make a
very positive impact on the life of a person with a disability.

In addition, social service agencies seem to place more emphasis on blood relationships than on friendships. If your child
with a disability might need to be involved with the social service
system after your death, a sibling can be an invaluable advocate
for him. In addition, courts often award guardianship to
siblings because of their long-term standing with the person
with the disability.

PARENT EXPECTATIONS

A social service group I belonged to was trying to decide whether or not to accept for membership a bright young woman who had a sister with mental retardation. One of the younger parents of a child with cognitive disabilities found out that the potential member almost never visited her sister, who lived at a private institution. The young parent was furious. An older parent of two adult women, one of whom has cerebral palsy, argued that this was not a reason to exclude the potential member. She argued, "Is some group going to discriminate against Marian [her non-disabled daughter] because she doesn't visit her sister enough? I don't want her saddled with that!"

Parents have different perceptions of the role of siblings in the future of their children with disabilities. Many overlook, or even discourage, the involvement of siblings because they don't want to place a hardship or burden on them. Other parents want the siblings to step right into the parents' role, doing things the way the parents would. Sometimes siblings will embrace these roles and sometimes parents' expectations can do more harm than good.

It may seem admirable to spare your other children the responsibility of caring for a person with a disability. However, as with other people, how your other children view your disabled son or daughter will probably have a lot to do with the image you are projecting.

Once again, if you see your child as a "burden on society," chances are, so will the sibling. If you see your 25-year-old adult son as a sort of overgrown child, his sister probably will, too. Don't be surprised to hear some of these same descriptions coming from your nondisabled child when he's introducing his brother to friends. Likewise, if you are always careful to talk about your child in respectful terms, the sibling probably will too.

When siblings have had the chance to develop their own relationship with the person with a disability, they may have a radically different view of what their brother or sister wants or needs. For example, a teenager may see that his slightly older brother with a disability would love to go to a rock concert. Their parents may think rock concerts are too sophisticated for the son with the disability or simply may not have thought about the possibility at all. Such insights can be extremely valuable to your planning; the trick is to develop the type of relationship that allows the sibling to share these views freely, enabling you to adjust your own perspectives and incorporating resulting suggestions into your plan for expanding networks.

Talking to your children can be difficult and developing an open relationship with them is not always easy. There are several good books on the market which can give you some assistance in this area; my favorite is *How To Talk So Kids Will Listen and Listen So Kids Will Talk* by Adele Faber and Elaine Mazlish. Basically, it suggests listening without being judgmental and acknowledging the child's feelings. I think the most important thing is to spend the time necessary to find out how each child feels. Time and a few good communication skills should help you unravel most problems.

Experts have found that siblings of people with cognitive disabilities are often very interested in being involved with their brother or sister throughout their lives. They may be unsure of what form their role should take, or they may be confused by mixed messages they receive from parents. Most children love their brothers and sisters, so it's a good bet that you may already have a strong ally in your efforts to expand your child's social network.

Parents often work hard to keep siblings' lives separate. Perhaps they feel that the age gap between siblings is too wide, or simply that kids with disabilities should be separate from nondisabled kids. If you have deliberately been keeping your children apart, for whatever reason, you are not going to be able to bring them closer together over night. You may need to be very patient in encouraging your nondisabled children to adopt a new role. Listen, listen, listen to the siblings when they talk about their brother or sister. What sounds like an initial strong negative reaction to getting more involved with their brother or sister may be a fear that they will not be able to do what's required and an awareness that they may need to be more responsible than usual in looking out for their sibling with the disability.

To help your other children see the positive side of having a sibling with disabilities, you must be patient. Involve siblings in your child's life gradually and with activities that are fun, depending upon the age of each. Ideally, you should start this process from birth. Take all your children to the park. If one of your nondisabled children has a sleep-over, include the sibling with the disability. There are a lot of possibilities for activities at any given age, but expect that older children will want to do some things separately. You need to respect this desire. If you do, the time that they spend together will be much more pleasant.

If your children have reached adulthood, they may have years of messages and experiences to overcome. Adult siblings will question whether or not they can care for their brother or sister with disabilities, sometimes because they have been receiving messages from parents that they are not competent to provide such care. They may also be under the impression that caring for a person with a disability is a one-way street with no rewards or benefits for the caretaker. Again, the best strategy is to bring the sibling into the process gradually. Increase his or her contact, perhaps through dinners together, or encourage a joint activity such as going to the movies once a month or taking a class at the local community center.

It may be upsetting to hear what siblings have to say about your child with a disability. They may reject their brother or sister totally, saying they are just too busy, or they may be highly critical of the way you've managed things so far. It will be important for everyone for you to keep your anger in check and your disappointment low-key. The first key to improving family dynamics is to listen openly and without criticism. Be open minded about the role that siblings will play in the life of your child with the disability. Although they may not initially choose the role you are hoping they will, in the long run it may very well turn out to be a valuable role. Remember, too, that relationships can change over time.

NEW PERSPECTIVES

"My eighteen-year-old daughter and her boyfriend took my son, Mike, hiking. I was really concerned about this; Mike has cerebral palsy so I thought hiking might be too frustrating for him. To my surprise, Mike came back muddy and sweaty but pleased with himself. Jennifer said that he crossed a stream on all fours. She said that it was hard for him and that he got tired, but he wanted to see it through. I could tell she was impressed."

❖

"When my son Donald turned 31 we had to place him in a state institution. We were just getting too old and he was getting more aggressive. We just couldn't handle it anymore. His younger brother, Frank, never had much to do with Donald, but said last year that he wanted to visit Donald at the institution. They got together for a couple of visits and then Frank started taking him out. The staff were real nervous; they were afraid that Donald would attack Frank. Frank said he didn't care and just kept taking him out. Donald did scratch him up a couple of times but Frank just shrugged it off. He said he thought Donald was `stressed out' over living in that place. Anyway, somewhere along the line, Frank got the idea that Donald was interested in music and he took him to the symphony. Can you believe that? They got all dressed up, Frank got really good seats, and off they went. Frank's talking about getting season tickets now! Who would have thought? I didn't even know Frank liked classical music!"

Siblings often seem to be better risk takers than parents. At a minimum, they can bring a fresh perspective and a new approach to expanding social networks. They often have a better sense of what people that age like and how they dress, and may do a better job of improving the person's image so that he fits into society better.

> "I started talking to Monica about Karyn's lack of friends. Monica is fourteen and her sister with Down syndrome is twelve. Monica just looked at me and said, 'Well what do you expect, Mom, you dress her like a dork!' I thought I had been doing a pretty good job, but Monica pointed out that the stuff I was picking out was too childish. So I took a big leap of faith and gave Monica control over Karyn's clothing budget. They shop together and Monica is very good about making sure Karyn likes what's being chosen. They started running into Monica's friends at the mall and Monica has started showing off her sister's clothes. Last week, I saw all of them, Karyn included, in a little pack laughing and talking in the food court. Letting Monica do this was the best thing I ever did."

It's important to let your children feel their own way in a relationship. Monica's mother would probably never have come up with the idea of clothes shopping as a way to get her two daughters together, but what a natural way for teenage girls to spend their time! Karyn not only enjoys a more fashionable, up-to-date teenage image, but she's also meeting new friends who probably would all like to give her some fashion tips.

PROBLEMS

> "I don't know. I've brought up the idea of Barry and Kevin spending more time together, but they're not going for it. Barry, my nondisabled child, just acts kind of sullen and says he doesn't want to. Kevin seemed interested at first, but now he says he doesn't want to either. He's even started taking Barry's stuff

> *without permission, something that really gets on*
> *Barry's nerves. Should I keep pushing?"*

Probably not. It seems that both children are feeling put upon and
Kevin is probably feeling some of his brother's negative reactions.
It would be helpful if you could get some idea what Barry's reser-
vations are, again by patiently identifying his underlying feelings
and reserving judgement. Remember, however, that all kids go
through phases of not wanting to share things with their parents.
You may want to let both children know that you still love them
despite their current problems with each other and periodically
suggest joint activities.

One nice thing about children, they will often see things entirely differently at different times. You will probably get plenty of
chances to try some gentle suggestions to get them together again.
You may want to take them both out to see a movie that they're
dying to see or go to a ball game if that's a big treat. Bill it as a family
outing and take some of the pressure off the boys to "socialize."

> *"I'm so disappointed in my daughter, Elizabeth. She's*
> *got everything going for her—nice husband, two*
> *great kids, a big house in the country, good job. I*
> *asked her to do one thing for her sister, Marsha, and*
> *she can't be bothered! She told me that she wasn't*
> *going to waste her life like I did and she wasn't 'into*
> *being a martyr.' I couldn't believe it. And what was*
> *worse, she was really mad that I would even bother*
> *to ask her. What's going on?"*

It's hard to say. Family dynamics are very complicated and it could
take a great deal of time and communication to find out what's
bothering your daughter. She could be feeling overburdened
by her family already or she could be really angry with you for
the way you've managed her sister's life so far. What you can do
is try to keep your anger in check, and look for an opportunity
to find out more about why Elizabeth is so upset. Perhaps it's
a simple misunderstanding that a talk can clear up, or maybe it's
a really serious divergence in viewpoints. Some families have
problems because the siblings feel cheated. They feel that the par-

ents focused all their attention on the child with the disability and gave nothing to them. Some families are able to resolve these issues by going through family counseling or by just talking them out; others are unable to resolve the problem. Again, be patient: today's situation may not be tomorrow's reality. You may get another chance.

Keep in mind that you are usually more likely to get a positive response from siblings if they know exactly what's needed to support their brother or sister and how to provide it. For example, when Samuel was born, he had some complications that resulted in severe brain injury. When he was three years old, he had to be fitted with a feeding tube and leg braces. His parents were reluctant to let his older sister, Katherine, touch him or even play with him. It was as if there were two different families living in the same house—one with Samuel and the other with Katherine. On several occasions, Katherine said that she felt cheated out of her parents' attention because of the time they devoted to Samuel.

Finally, when Katherine was sixteen and Samuel was nine, the family decided that Mom would have to take a full-time job to make ends meet. After trying for months to find a reliable person to take care of Samuel after school, the mother blurted out her frustration to Katherine. Katherine said that she would be willing to help, but needed to know exactly what to do. Her mother showed her, and with some hesitation, left Samuel with Katherine for the afternoon. She returned to find both children happy and satisfied with the new arrangement. Katherine has since told her mother that she had always been fascinated by Samuel but felt that he was somehow "off limits" to her. Now Katherine has decided that she wants to go to college to become a physical therapist.

> "My son, Justin, is a yes man. He agrees to everything that I ask him to do with his sister, Amy. He never complains. I don't think it's normal. I feel that I may be asking too much of him, making him more of an adult than he needs to be right now, but he says not."

Parents know their children best. If you think Justin is just saying yes out of some sense of duty, you might look for ways to build more give-and-take into the relationship between him and Amy. Are there too many joint activities geared to Amy's interests rather than Justin's? Try adjusting the balance. You might also try offering him some one-on-one time with a parent to see what kinds of things he really likes to do. Justin needs to get the message that while you are thrilled with his relationship with his sister, he needs to pay attention to his own needs too. Most siblings will naturally work out a healthy balance between the two.

WHAT ABOUT THE LONG-TERM VIEW?

Even if your children get along great and their relationship is everything you could want, I think it's a mistake to assume that the nondisabled sibling(s) will care for his brother or sister with a disability after you die. At least not in the same way you did. Children are just like anyone else; they grow up, get married, and have careers and children—all of which take their time and energy. In addition, children are not guaranteed immortality when their parents die. As unpleasant as it is to think about, your other child could become disabled or sick or could die, leaving no one to look out for your child with the disability.

If you have more than two children, you obviously have more options. Make sure, however, that you're not relying on one nondisabled sibling too heavily—the only unmarried daughter, for instance. Some families divide up the responsibilities; a brother may have the sibling with the disability move in with his family, while an accountant sister handles all the financial duties.

There are no legal obligations that a sibling must take care of a brother or sister with a disability, and unless stipulated in a will or trust, no financial obligations either. Any commitments made will be moral ones. That's one reason why it's best to try to work out some arrangements before you die. For more on exactly what to do and say, see Chapter 9.

Even if your nondisabled child is not going to be the primary caretaker for your child with the disability, you will want to make sure that he or she knows where all your child's records are, what financial arrangements have been made, who the primary caretaker will be, etc. Knowing all this in advance will make for an easier transition when the time comes. And make sure that the primary caretaker welcomes the assistance and guidance of the sibling. As mentioned before, probably no one else knows your child better. Usually, siblings have a good sense of your child's history and know what has worked in the past and what hasn't. If the primary caretaker isn't willing to work with the siblings, that's something that you need to consider further. Siblings, regardless of whether or not they will be the primary caretaker, are an important part of your child's network.

> *"Recently, my husband's boss died unexpectedly and we had to go out of town for a few days. Our normal sitter was not available so we had to leave Sam with his brother, Paul. I was really worried. Paul has never taken care of Sam, and Sam has profound mental retardation with seizures, toileting problems, the whole works. I was pleasantly surprised to find out that they had no problems. Paul handled everything beautifully. He even offered to take care of Sam anytime we needed!"*

Sometimes, we still think of our children as being less capable than they really are, whether they have disabilities or not. Whatever your children's current relationship, it may be wise to at least entertain the possibility of involving siblings more in your child's life. More often than not, you will be pleasantly surprised at the results.

CHAPTER 7

HOW DO I MAKE
THINGS HAPPEN?

I f you've been following the suggestions in this book
so far, you should be armed with the following:

- ✐ Your vision of the future;
- ✐ Your son's or daughter's interest in and
  agreement to work on the situation;
- ✐ An understanding of your child's interests, gifts, and abilities;
- ✐ A list of community opportunities to
  meet people, and/or a list of people who
  can help with the process;
- ✐ A commitment to work on expanding
  your child's social network as much as
  possible, promoting every promising
  opportunity for friendship.

Now comes the nitty gritty work of making some new friends. The first step is to choose which approach you would like to try first—joining a group or talking to a key person who can introduce your child to other potential friends. Here are some ideas for both approaches.

TALKING TO A KEY PERSON

1. Introduce yourself to the person, if necessary, and schedule an opportunity to meet. This can involve a formal appointment, like meeting over lunch, or simply scheduling some time for yourself to get to the library or wherever the person happens to be.

2. Explain what your child is interested in, like art or cooking, and explain that she wants to meet other people with the same interests. Make sure that you explain your child's skill level. If she wants to learn basic computer skills, make sure she doesn't get hooked up with people who want to become computer programmers.

3. Try to enlist the person's agreement to help. You may want to give just a basic explanation of what your child will need— for example, someone to watch so she knows what to do, a ride to the activity, or someone who will answer her questions and show her around. I think it helps to be as concrete as possible. At minimum, you want to come away from the discussion with names of other people who would be interested in assisting your child. If the key person volunteers his own assistance, and he's a stranger, you will probably want to join in the activities until you get to know him.

Occasionally, you'll find someone who seems to have no ideas. You may want to just move on to the next person. Or you may want to quiz a little bit further. Here's a sample conversation:

> "My daughter, Jill, is interested in taking a painting course. She would need a beginner's class. Do you know of any?"
>
> "No, I don't."
>
> "How about a local artist? Do you know of anyone who paints professionally?"

"No."
"Do they offer classes at the high school?"
"I don't know."
"Do you know someone I could ask over there?"
"No, but here's a number you can call."
"Thanks."

If you have a conversation like this, you probably didn't choose your key person well. You want someone who is well connected and knows what the community has to offer. A librarian, a community center director, a newspaper reporter, someone in the mayor's office—these are the types of people who know a lot about your community and could be useful for this first step. Don't expect that everyone will know what clubs and activities are available. Don't be discouraged either. There are plenty of contacts out there. If you fail with your first attempt, go on to the next.

At this stage, be careful not to limit options for your child. Once you have identified a particular activity or group to join, then you can look into how to modify it. Try to approach a potential activity with an attitude of "I know it can work" before you give up on an idea. Don't assume that a particular activity won't be beneficial to your child just because she has a cognitive disability. Don't let your "key person" limit your child's options either. For example:

*"I'm looking for a beginner's painting class for my
    daughter, Jill."*
*"Since Jill has Down syndrome, you may want to contact
    Happy Sunrise camp. They do some great things over
    there for special people."*
*"Well, we really wanted to try something different. Jill's
    very interested in water colors and would like to take
    a regular class."*
*"Well, there's a painter in town who gives lessons, but I'm
    not sure she'd take Jill."*
*"Why don't you give me her name, and I'll work out the
    details."*
"Okay. . . ."

The examples above are offered in case you meet with resistance. Happily though, the Americans with Disabilities Act has made many people more sensitive to the needs of people with disabilities. People are often more open-minded now about who can participate in community activities. You will probably come across people who are more than happy to help.

I have personally witnessed people learning to be more sensitive and aware of people with disabilities. In one instance, I supported someone with mental retardation who was taking an extremely rigorous values clarification (personal ethics) course in college. The instructor for the course told me that he had concerns about a person with mental retardation participating; the material was highly intellectual. But my friend, Ray, and I both finished that course and learned a lot. I really enjoyed helping him, because I had to take all the jargon that was being tossed around and explain it to him in simple, concrete terms. Ray felt good about his participation, and found that the course challenged a lot of assumptions he made about other people. After it was all over, the instructor came back to Ray and said he had been wrong. Ray had every right to be in that group, and it was an important lesson for all of us.

A similar change of attitudes occurred when a group of people with cognitive disabilities in Pennsylvania decided that they wanted to attend classes at a local community college. Each of them agreed to pay the tuition for someone who could assist them in attending the class. The nondisabled students would drive the students with disabilities, hang out with them, and help explain difficult parts of the courses. The idea worked really well, and many of the "helpers" afterwards said that it really helped them to help someone else. They better understood the course material and learned a great deal about people with disabilities in the process.

4. Introduce your child to the potential friend, as suggested by the key person. If the other person doesn't know how to react, be a good role model. Don't apologize for your child. Model respectful behavior. Talk to your child, not around her. Lead the way, and encourage your contact to ask questions. It's the only way people are going to learn.

I personally would not mention my child's disability label, such as Down syndrome or cerebral palsy. Kierkegaard said, "If you label me, you negate me." I tend to agree, though I recognize instances when descriptions are helpful. I just don't think labels go very far in really explaining what your child wants or needs when you are talking to a typical person. It might be better to enlist the person's help in a very practical way, saying something like, "I'm looking for some people who would want to do arts and crafts with my eight-year-old. She needs a place where she can walk around the room a lot. Can you think of anyone I can talk to? Would you arrange a meeting?"

Once you are in a setting where your child needs assistance, you may want to make suggestions about modifying activities to your child's skill level or give some tips on managing different behaviors. For example, if your child has an attention deficit disorder, you might want to ask if she could sit in the front of the class to minimize distractions. If you think your child will need many special accommodations, you and your child may want to meet with the instructor or club president ahead of time to make sure everything is in place.

JOINING A GROUP

1. Attend a meeting or visit the organization. Talk to members about your son's or daughter's interest in joining.

2. Have your son or daughter attend.

3. Do whatever it takes to help ensure that it's a positive experience for everyone. Again, you may want to make some practical suggestions to appropriate group members on how to make the meeting successful for your child. You might request materials ahead of time so that you can review them with your child before the meeting, or you might want to suggest to your child that she volunteer for some important detail like setting up coffee and bringing donuts. There will be hundreds of ways to make attendance at a meeting an enjoyable experience. If you get stumped, ask the group leader for suggestions.

NOTE: Many parents I know take their son or daughter with them the first time. If this works for you, great! If it doesn't seem to be going as well as it should, you may want to leave. Later you could return alone to feel out the situation, then relay what you've learned to your son or daughter. Some people with disabilities feel more comfortable if they have an idea of what's going to happen at a meeting before they actually attend.

Participating in the Group

Some parents need to nudge their children to speak up at meetings. This can be because of communication difficulties (it's just too much work) or because of shyness. Parents are usually good at knowing how much to push their child and when to lay back. One of my children is very shy at first; in new situations, I let him just wander around and watch what's happening. After a short time, he's usually comfortable and begins to open up on his own. He doesn't respond well if I push him.

My other child likes to be the center of attention, but may not know how to make his first move in a new setting. He looks to me for signals. I'll invite him into a conversation by saying something like, "Why don't you tell George about your hockey game?" and he's off and running. Most of the time, though, he'll seize the initiative and go up to some new kid and say, "Hi, do you want to play?"

My point is that you need to follow your instincts about how much to push your child. If I push my shy son too hard, the day becomes disastrous. Sometimes, I have to rein my other child in because he's too sociable, and we would have dozens of kids at the house at all hours. You know your kid. Follow your instincts.

Sometimes, it may be hard to figure out just how someone with a disability can contribute to a group. This can be hard for anyone, not only people with disabilities. I usually volunteer for the jobs nobody else seems to want: flipping sausages at the annual fundraising breakfast, stuffing envelopes, putting labels on newsletters, sitting on the bylaws committee. There are jobs like this in any association or club, and they may be good ways for a person with a disability to get acclimated to the group.

FAMILY TO FAMILY

This book focuses on two primary means of expanding your child's social contacts: by joining a group or by talking with a key person. It is worth mentioning, however, that there are other good ways of helping your child make friends. This includes making the process a family affair.

Tom's family built an elaborate wooden fort in their backyard. The neighborhood kids love to climb all over the fort, and are always happy to visit with Tom. Another family I know has regular pool parties for the neighborhood. Still another family with a disabled family member organized a block party to help all of their neighbors get to know each other better. Now, the neighbors take time to chat with each other regularly, extending the same courtesy to the person with the disability as well.

You might want to take a cue from these families and work on building relationships for your whole family rather than just for your child with a disability. For instance, you may want to host regular open house get-togethers, organize Christmas caroling for the neighborhood, or ask one other family along on a camping trip, a visit to the zoo or amusement park, or on some other activity that can be enjoyed by all ages.

When your child participates as part of your family, it can take a lot of tension and pressure off of everyone. Your child can be seen as a capable and accepted member of your family, and others can model their interactions with her on those of you and your children. You can help guide others' perceptions of your child by assigning her responsibilities that will show her in a good light. For example, if you give a party, you can have her make sure everyone has something to drink, take everyone's coat, or answer the door when someone knocks. Give her a job that is routine and easy, but gives her the opportunity to come in contact with everyone.

TURNING ACQUAINTANCES INTO FRIENDS

Sooner or later, you and your child will want to make some of her relationships deeper and more intimate. By this I mean moving them from the status of acquaintances met once a week or once a month to the status of "good friend."

Usually, it will be obvious who your child likes in a group. It's a myth that people with cognitive disabilities like all people indiscriminately. Everyone I know with a cognitive disability clearly likes some people and not others. Even if your child is non-verbal, you'll see who your child feels comfortable with, likes to sit near, etc. In the rare instance that you can't tell which group member(s) should be targeted for a closer relationship, you may want to allow more time for things to develop. You may also want to see who expresses the most interest in your son or daughter. Many times, these will be people whom your child likes as well.

The best way to help your child make friends is to think about ways *you* have made friends. Perhaps you seemed to hit it off with someone you met. After a couple of meetings, the good feelings continued and you decided that you wanted to get to know this person outside of the group. Your next step may have been to invite the person to a party with your friends or to some other kind of group activity. Or you may have plunged right in and invited the person to something one-on-one: a lunch date, an outing, or a visit to your home. It is also possible to take more gradual steps, such as calling the person on the phone between meetings, lending the person a CD or video, sharing a snack, sending greeting cards, volunteering to work with the person on a related project, asking him or her for help in understanding a group issue, etc. You can then gauge the person's reactions, looking for signs that the relationship will or won't work. Whichever approach you and your child decide upon is fine, as long as it seems natural and comfortable to both of you.

If your child is shy or doesn't communicate in typical ways, you may need to provide some assistance to get things rolling. One mom I know always makes sure that her son brings nice little party favors for all the kids when he's invited to someone's house. This helps break the ice for Jake, who can be a little difficult to understand. She also frequently volunteers to have group activities at her house, which is another way to give people a chance to get to know her son.

Other parents make sure to send cards or birthday gifts at the appropriate time. One mom carpools to ballet class so that her daughter with mental retardation gets that extra time with nondisabled kids.

Conversation 101

New Hats, Inc., the organization mentioned in Chapter Four, has done considerable work helping people to expand their social networks and make some of those relationships more intimate. Their guide, "Using Natural Supports in Community Integration," includes a "Conversation Start Up Kit" which tells people how to make the acquaintance of someone they would like to meet. These suggestions are particularly useful if your child is shy or approaches people inappropriately.

RIDING ON A BUS

Conversation with a stranger:
1. Does this bus stop at _____ Street? Thank you.
2. Pardon me. Could you tell me what time it is? (or some other information query) Thanks. I was wondering if I would be late for my appointment.
3. How do you like the weather today? I like it because _____.
OR I don't like it because _____. I hope it changes tomorrow. OR I hope it stays the same tomorrow.

Conversation with someone you want to get to know better:
1. I sure like that _____ you have. I've been looking for something like that; where did you get it?
2. Would you mind if I sit by you? OR May I please sit by you? OR I'd like to sit here, would you mind? (If no) Thanks anyway. (smile) Oh. Well then, I'll sit over here.
3. I noticed that you ride this bus everyday. Do you enjoy it? OR Where do you get off the bus?

IN A STORE, LIBRARY, OR RESTAURANT

Conversation with a stranger:

1. Do you now if there's a restroom here? (OR drinking fountain OR a public telephone). Thank you.
2. Do you know where the _____ are located (example: crackers) (further description) You know, the kind that _____. I need them for _____.
3. Could you help me with something? I need (OR I want) to go to the 3rd floor, and I don't know where the escalator is. (checking out or clarifying) Oh, do you mean _____?
OR I think I know what you mean; you mean _____.
OR Is this what you're saying? Is this the right direction?

Conversation with someone you want to know better:

1. Do you happen to know anything about _____ (a product)? I'm trying to decide between _____ and _____, and I don't know which to choose.
2. Did you notice that oranges are on sale today for 25 cents a pound? OR How do you like the new shopping carts? (something unique or appealing or interesting, a change, a hot tip)
3. Do you know when this place closes? Do you know, is there a bus stop (OR coffee shop) nearby?

AT A CHURCH, SCHOOL, SOCIAL, OR SPORTS GATHERING

Conversation with a stranger:

1. Is there a _____ nearby? (7-Eleven, drug store, bus stop, a subway, pencil sharpener, coat room, a coat rack)
2. Is it OK if I _____? (sing loud, go in late, leave early, bring a guest, go dressed like this, don't have the right change, haven't got a ticket/reservation)
3a. Do you know where I can get a _____? (hymn book, a coke, some popcorn, some refreshments, program,)
3b. Would you mind showing me? (pointing it out?) OR Would you consider going there with me?

Conversation with someone you see often and want to know better:
1. May I have a copy of _____? OR Is it OK if I copy _____?
(your speech, your poem, the article, your idea, the instructions,
directions, the assignment, the schedule, your map)
2. Do you have _____ I could borrow?
OR May I borrow _____? (a pocket knife, a pen, pencil,
a pad to write on, a nickel, quarter, your binoculars, a needle,
a flashlight, your book, tape)
3. Could I have _____? (your telephone number,
address, another chance, 15 minutes of your time, your bracelet
to look at [purse, ID card, ring, scarf, glove, briefcase], one of
your flowers, a kleenex, some tape, a paper clip)
4. Would you be willing to share your _____? (bench, table,
blanket, peanuts, popcorn, water, pew, program, sandwich,
locker, newspaper, hand lotion)
5. I'd like to _____, if that's o.k. with you? (save you a
seat, call you sometime, come over to see you, see you again)

It's best to use these suggestions as idea generators for role
playing rather than rote responses to situations. Have your child
pretend that you're the person she'd like to invite to a party, or
get to know better. Then act out a variety of responses, positive
and negative, and give her pointers on what to do next. The suggested phrases are intended to give you and your child concrete
ideas on how to approach someone. They should be considered
launching points for new friendships, not complete interactions
by themselves.

Relationship Mechanics

Considering their long history of social isolation, it is not surprising that many people with disabilities do not know how to manage
a relationship. In fact, this is such a common problem that a recent study found it was the number one reason that people with
mental retardation failed on the job. They failed not because of
poor job skills, but because of a lack of social skills.

Problems with relationship "mechanics" may surface not just on the job, but in other situations as well. Remembering birthdays, sending a thank-you note, or just knowing how to act with a friend may be areas in which you can assist. You may also want to help your child identify things she can do to show a new friend appreciation or interest. New Hats, Inc. has the following ideas on how to support and nurture relationships:

Taking Care of Relationships

Maintain them by:
- communicating
- taking, finding time
- staying in touch
- timely meddling, sensitive probing
- offering empathy during crises
- sharing resources, ideas
- being realistic in giving
- opening to forgiveness
- noticing the gifts that giving brings

Deepen them by:
- examining values
- working through problems
- allowing feelings - anger, grief, joy, fear
- discovering the opportunities in challenges
- sharing laughter and tears
- playing together
- listening deeply
- sharing dreams and hopes
- exchanging affection
- making commitments
- verifying confidentiality, loyalty
- being spontaneous

Honor them by:
- valuing change
- being honest

- saying yes or no and meaning it
- expressing appreciation and affection
- acknowledging each person's contribution
- having preferences and priorities rather than expectations and demands
- giving attention to personal gifts and surprises
- celebrating accomplishments, special days
- loving myself
- creating a better world
- being responsible for own feelings, thoughts, and actions

These suggestions may seem a little abstract, but they should start you thinking about all the little things that make relationships work. You could remind your son or daughter to ask friends how they are feeling or to say that they appreciate the time spent together. We all tend to take such things for granted, but they are really important in bonding people together.

Overcoming Negative Experiences

The best way to learn how to be a friend is "in vivo" or actually within a friendship. People with disabilities may need encouragement to overcome reactions born of their past negative experiences with friendships. For example, some people with disabilities are so lonely and so desperate for someone to care about them that they over commit to someone they have met on a casual basis. They might just be a little overly familiar with a stranger, or they might go so far as to give money and possessions to someone they barely know.

> Joe met John when he went to the diner for breakfast the first time. He called him "buddy" and tried to strike up a conversation. John was uncomfortable with this, and after repeated attempts at ignoring Joe, rudely told him to mind his own business. Joe was hurt but focused his attention on teasing the waitresses. Joe kept going to the diner and so did John. After about two weeks they seemed to get used to each other. Now, Joe says "Hi, buddy" and John responds as if he's genuinely glad to see Joe.

If your child is overly friendly, it is important to try to understand the reasons behind her behavior. Perhaps she has not had a satisfactory number of relationships. If she is not skilled at reading interpersonal cues, she will need more practice to learn what's appropriate and what's not.

Sometimes someone may behave in an overly friendly way because it was acceptable in another setting. For example, I knew a woman named Nancy who would run up to any stranger and throw her arms around him and give him a big bear hug. She would also adopt a high-pitched squeal and ask the person questions in a babyish voice, though she was in her thirties. I found out that she used to live in a state institution where many of the residents used to do the same thing. They saw so few visitors that it was a major event when someone new actually came. Nancy eventually changed her behavior with a lot of advice and encouragement. It also helped that she saw strangers every day in her new life in a group home. She got a lot of messages from these strangers about what was acceptable and what wasn't.

If your child has a similar problem, expose her to as many different people as possible, and she will usually develop appropriate ways of dealing with them. It may take some time and watchfulness on your part, but this is usually the best approach. If you find this strategy embarrassing, I encourage you to overcome your embarrassment and brazen it out. Your child will likely pick up on your embarrassment, which may provide another signal to her to modify her behavior. If this is simply impossible, delegate the task to someone else—a family member, friend, or perhaps even a professional whose sole responsibility it is to introduce your child to others and help her develop better social skills.

Sometimes people with disabilities take the opposite approach to relationships. They are overly sensitive to signs of rejection and try to shut down a promising opportunity.

Bob was an avid gardener and worked diligently on maintaining his gorgeous flower beds. His neighbor, Matt, admired Bob's work on several occasions and asked if Bob could give him some pointers. Bob declined. When asked about his decision later on, Bob said it didn't make sense to make friends with Matt; he would probably move away like his other friends had.

Several things could be done to assist Bob in getting over his reticence about meeting new people. You could invite Matt over yourself and work Bob into the conversation, or you could address the problem head on and talk with Bob about ways to keep up contacts when and if Matt should move away. It's important to recognize, though, that Bob is probably speaking from experience. Years of hurt and disappointment need to be overcome. It's natural that he would be a little reluctant to continually pursue relationships. Any agreements you make with him must therefore be kept if he is going to overcome this reluctance.

Assisting from the Sidelines

Setting a Good Example

When helping people meet your son or daughter, you may have to provide the nondisabled person with support as well. Some people are interested but unsure as to how to be a friend to a person with a disability. Again the best way to learn is "in vivo." However there are some things you can keep in mind. When the two are in your presence, you will want to model for the friend how to relate to your child. If you talk to your adult child in a patronizing way or as if she were two years old, don't be surprised to see her new friend talk to her in the same way. If you introduce your child as a "CP" or a "victim of Down syndrome" don't be surprised when new friends introduce her the same way. The relationship will have much more balance and a better chance for reciprocity and longevity if you talk to your child as an equal with all the respect and dignity that you reserve for your friends.

Offering Suggestions

Things can and will go wrong. Most times, if given the opportunity, the parties in the relationship will work things out on their own. For example, in the story of Joe and John, mentioned earlier, Joe adjusted by not focusing so much attention on John, and John became a little friendlier. This was a relatively minor problem, but community members have demonstrated a wonderful ability to deal with all kinds of difficulties. Sometimes they may need some assistance from you. You may want to let them know what kinds of situations increase your son's or daughter's stress. Or you might tell them that it's okay to set guidelines for the relationship, such as "please don't call me at the office, only at home."

Dealing with Prejudice

Connie's son, Ben, had just gotten a job doing mainte-nance at their church. The pastor knew that Ben has mental retardation and asked to have a meeting with Connie and the church elders to iron out any possible problems. During the meeting, one woman said that she thought it wouldn't work out because the children in Sunday School would tease Ben about being mentally retarded. Connie said that she and Ben both knew that he might be teased and that they would handle the situation if and when it arose. The church elders were reluctant but finally agreed to give Ben a chance. The children never did tease Ben and didn't even seem to think that there was anything different about him.

Parents get really worked up about the possibility that their child will be teased. And it certainly is a possibility. After all, there probably aren't too many people who haven't been teased for one reason or another. Except for severe cases, however, most people who are teased survive. In Ben's case, a fear of teasing could have cost him a job. It's great that he and his mother knew that teasing was a risk of making new acquaintances and decided to try anyway.

Unfortunately, there are a few people who have a bias against people with disabilities that they are not going to be able to over-come. Such people, while they may pop up in your child's life more frequently than anyone likes, are usually in the minority. Most people who are initially uncomfortable around people with disabilities get over this discomfort as they get to know the indi-vidual. There are really very few who won't give your child a chance.

If you do come across someone who is truly prejudiced, he or she may try to bar your child's access to an important service or even employment. If this is the case, please realize that you probably have some legal remedy available to you. Sometimes it may be better just to try another opportunity for meeting people. What I would hate to have happen is for the person with the disability to assume that all people in the community are bad and go back to a life of very limited social contacts. Please encourage your child to keep trying and to focus on the positive relationships in her life.

If your child has suffered some kind of rejection or attack, sympathize as you would with anyone. You may want to say something like, "Boy, when she called you that name, you got your feelings hurt." As discussed in previous chapters, you can encourage your child to open up to you by helping her identify the emotion or feeling that went along with the experience.

Helping a Child Who Lives Away from Home

If your child lives away from home in some kind of residential program, you may have to work with staff to ensure that they help support any budding friendships. Oftentimes, they will be happy to do any of the things we mentioned above to help a relationship develop. If so, great! If not, again try to work with the administration to see that your son or daughter can have unlimited access to the friend and vice versa.

You may want to have it written into your child's program plan that the relationship is supported through a variety of ways: regular phone calls, frequent outings, sending cards on birthdays and holidays, etc. Finally, if it's feasible, you may want to assume a supporting role by doing any of the things already mentioned, along with providing transportation to outings and encouraging the friend to maintain contact despite any problems with the staff.

Respecting Your Child's Taste in Friends

Not surprisingly, parents and their children sometimes disagree about who makes a good friend. Although you may feel compelled to convince your child to drop someone as a friend, consider how you would handle this situation with someone who did not have a disability. It may be better to keep your opinions to yourself or to make some minimal comments about why you would not pursue the person as a friend. As we discussed before, the chemistry that makes for a good relationship is a mysterious thing; the kind of people who make you feel good may be totally different from the type of people who make your son or daughter feel good.

TROUBLESHOOTING RELATIONSHIPS

"I've being doing this stuff for awhile now, and it seems like my kid never makes any friends. She signs up for a lot of different activities and seems to enjoy himself, but doesn't have any new relationships. What's wrong?"

This can be frustrating. Sometimes, it's simply that you and your child have a different idea of what constitutes a "friend." You may want to quiz her a little bit more, asking if there is someone she always sits with, talks to, etc. Other times, there may be problems with the activity itself. For example, it could be so boring that people can't wait for it to be over. Or it may be something that your daughter is

PROBLEMS MAKING FRIENDS

❑ **Is the relationship between your child and the other person unbalanced?** For example, does your child expect too much and give too little in return?

❑ **Are there too few mutual interests?** e.g., is there too big a difference in age, or in skills?

❑ **Is this an activity *your child* really wants to do, or is it something you want her to do?**

❑ **Is the activity long enough to encourage the development of a relationship?** Is it something that occurs over several weeks or regularly enough to allow your child to get to know someone?

❑ **Do the same people tend to participate, or are there different people every time?**

❑ **Are there breaks, joint projects, or committees which allow people to talk with each other freely?**

❑ **Is the other person in the relationship mainly out of a sense of charity?**

doing that could be easily changed. In any event, below is a checklist to help you pinpoint where the problem may lie.

> *"My son has autism and doesn't like to be around anyone except his parents and his siblings. How is he possibly going to make friends with strangers?"*

Social contact is extremely challenging for many people with autism. However, it is critical that people with autism be able to make contact with someone besides family members, particularly if family members are older or are considering residential services for their child. I would recommend that you start with family activities, so that he can have the security of nearby parents and siblings but can also learn to tolerate other people. You will want to keep the activities structured and short, at first. If he's up to it, you may want to encourage him to play a game of catch or involve him in some other activity that requires everyone to take turns. If this is not a good idea, take everyone to a petting zoo or invite

❑ **Is the other person afraid to get close to your child?** (Perhaps because he sees your child as too needy or for other reasons?)

❑ **Is the other person too busy to take time to get to know your child?**

❑ **Are needed accommodations being made to allow your child to participate fully in the activity?** Is the activity leader a positive influence?

❑ **Could your presence be interfering with the development of friendships?** Do people tend to address questions to you rather than to your child when you're around? Do you do too much for your child, making it seem as if she's less capable and grown-up than she is?

❑ **Is your child projecting an attitude that is keeping others away?** e.g., is she acting like she doesn't want friends or is she acting immature?

❑ **Do you think that something is preventing the other person from seeing and appreciating your child's good qualities?** If so, see the next checklist on pages 114-15 for help in Removing Obstacles.

REMOVING OBSTACLES CHECKLIST

Why do you believe that others would enjoy being your child's friend? List what you consider to be the biggest reasons.

_____

_____

_____

_____

_____

_____

Are these reasons/qualities readily apparent to casual acquaintances?   ☐ Yes   ☐ No

If not, what prevents your child's positive qualities from being recognized?

☐ communication difficulties?

☐ poor social skills? (e.g., she stands too close to others, she talks too loudly, she doesn't make eye contact, she has "bad manners," etc.)

☐ lack of skills needed to participate in the activity?

☐ her personality? (e.g., she is very shy)

☐ her appearance/grooming? (e.g., she uses a wheelchair, which others may find off-putting; she has bad teeth)

☐ behavior problems? (e.g., aggressiveness, extreme hyperactivity)

☐ lack of self-esteem

☐ others' ignorance about disability issues in general or your child's disability in particular, i.e. prejudice

☐ others' inability to value these qualities (e.g., she may have a great sense of humor, but is involved with people who are working hard to solve a serious problem; or she is very talented artistically, but is not around art lovers)

❏ the setting doesn't allow these qualities to shine
❏ other things?

What can you do to remove each of these obstacles?

❏ Can you teach your child new skills by practicing more, watching films, getting her a mentor? Or, if your child is still in school, can you add these skills to her IEP? If your child receives rehabilitation services, can you add a goal to her IHP? Otherwise, is there a professional who could help? (Speech-language pathologist, social worker, psychologist, rehabilitation counselor, etc.)

❏ Have you ruled out medical reasons for strange behavior or grooming problems? Could she be having a hearing problem or need new glasses?

❏ Can you help her learn new ways of behavior? e.g., by explaining to your child how to behave, by role playing problem situations with her, or by arranging a signal with her to let her know when she is doing a problem behavior? If you can't change her behavior, can you get assistance from a professional?

❏ If there is something about your child that can't be changed, such as her basic personality, can you find settings/activities where her strengths will be more readily apparent? e.g., one-on-one or small group activities if your child is very shy; outdoor activities if your child is boisterous or needs to move around a lot, etc.

❏ Can you educate others about better ways to interact with your child?

❏ Can you try another class in a different location, with a more understanding group leader, with more time for discussion and small group projects?

people over for pizza. Host the activities in your own home, if possible, but make sure that your son can retreat to his room by himself if he feels the need. I personally would not be at all confrontational, but I would lavishly praise any eye contact or other attempts at connecting. As with any child, build on his strengths and interests. If these are not apparent to you, work harder at identifying them (review Chapter 4) or seek professional assistance.

> *"My child has multiple disabilities. She uses a wheelchair and has great difficulty communicating even the simplest thing. People tend to treat her as if she's not there. I've signed her up for all kinds of activities and nobody even talks to her, let alone tries to make friends with her."*

People are probably a little concerned that they may hurt or injure your daughter, or they are interpreting her difficulties in communication as a lack of interest. In this situation, someone needs to model for others how to best interact with your child. Work with the group leader to do this or attend the classes with your child yourself. If these suggestions fail, find a mentor for her within the group, or sign her up for the activity along with someone she already knows. Whoever attends with her can introduce her around and get a better idea of what the obstacle may be.

Before giving up on the activity, you could just ask someone in the class (assuming you've already asked your child and she has no idea!) what they think the problem is. This often works wonders. If not, try a different type of activity, such as family activities or something more individually designed.

> *"My son has been going to club meetings for three months. People are polite to him afterwards over snacks, but don't seem interested in being friends."*

Review the section on "Turning Acquaintances into Friends" for some ideas on how to get started. Work with your child on his skills in deepening relationships. It could be that three months just isn't enough time for your son and you need to be more patient with the process. If you disagree, you can do something to try to push the process along, such as attending a club meeting with him to get an idea of who the players are and what the problem may be. You can help him plan to host a meeting or party for the club at home. Meet with the club leader and see if you can come up with some ideas that would help him develop friendships. Can he serve on a committee? Distribute supplies, song books, etc. every week? Call roll? Lead the pledge to the flag? Bring donuts? Little things like this will help pave the way for him to increase his involvement and his friendships as well.

> *"Together, my child and I chose several activities for her to try. She says she has an OK time, but that she'd rather hang out with her friends (with disabilities). She says they're more fun to be with and don't have trouble understanding her. Now she doesn't want to try any more activities with nondisabled people."*

If your child has been participating in a segregated program for a long period of time, this could happen. I suggest a mix of segregated and non-segregated activities to start out. You may want to increase her comfort level with non-segregated activities by participating as an entire family, or by encouraging her to attend with a friend who also has disabilities.

You may also want to help her improve her communication skills. Perhaps she feels a little self-conscious about her speech. Speech therapy may make her feel more confident when talking with nondisabled people.

People with disabilities don't have some magical ability to understand each other. It's likely that her friends have probably just known her longer and that is why they can understand her more easily. If non-disabled people are given some time, they will probably be able to understand her too.

It would be a mistake, in my opinion, to give up entirely. Try some particularly enticing activity. Few professional wrestling fans can resist going to see a live show, and nearly everyone likes going out for pizza and a movie. And if you're home with her one day, what's to stop your friends from visiting you while she's there? Start over, think small, and introduce nondisabled people in easy-to-manage doses. Afterwards, compliment her on her ability to make chit-chat, or whatever. Reduce the pressure, but don't give up. She needs to have other people in her life.

ABUSIVE RELATIONSHIPS

"How do you know who to trust? There are so many weirdos around today. My daughter can't talk and I don't think she would be able to tell me if someone was abusing her. I'd like to see her have a lot of friends but I'm afraid someone is going to take advantage of her."

Unfortunately, abuse can happen, and parents are wise to be concerned about it. There are, however, some steps you can take to guard against it. Most importantly, if you have concerns about a particular relationship, you may want to look at it more objectively.

While everyone has a different idea of what makes a good friend, there are some common denominators. Some of these characteristics were listed in a guide called "People Do Matter: There Is No Excuse for Abuse," published by New York's Office of Mental Retardation and Developmental Disabilities. This guide provides useful information to social service administrators on how to identify and address possible incidents of abuse in their programs for people with mental retardation. The guide lists characteristics associated with positive and negative caregivers as one tipoff to the kind of relationship someone may have with a person with a disability. This list may help you assess the quality of your child's friendships, as well as help you put your finger on why you think there's a problem.

CHARACTERISTICS ASSOCIATED WITH POSITIVE CAREGIVING OR THOSE OF A GOOD FRIEND
(Use this list to assess the behavior of the nondisabled person in the relationship)
- trusting
- optimistic
- outgoing, easygoing, warmhearted
- uninhibited
- tenderminded

- mature and calm
- resourceful
- self-assured
- relaxed
- warm, compassionate, kind, sensitive
- sees others as capable & trustworthy
- empathic
- genuine
- self-revealing
- sees others as dependable
- sees others as able to direct their lives
- sees self as part of the masses
- sees self as adequate
- sees self as likeable, worthwhile
- concern for larger issues; gets involved

CHARACTERISTICS ASSOCIATED WITH NEGATIVE CAREGIVING (OR FRIENDSHIPS TO BE CONCERNED ABOUT)

- low self-esteem
- inability to cope under stress
- poor interpersonal relations
- impulsive
- suspicious
- rigid
- preference for structures and rules
- low empathy

If you think there is a problem with a relationship, talk to your child about your concerns. Use some of the above terms to help you describe what's missing. Chances are she feels that something isn't quite right, too, and she may just be looking for a graceful way to get out of the situation. If you are concerned that the relationship may be abusive, check your concerns against the characteristics listed in Appendix D. Then swiftly take whatever steps are necessary to stop the abuse. Get your child away from the abuser as soon as possible, either by stopping contact between the two or by calling the appropriate authorities for an investigation.

CONCLUSION

It's easy to get caught up in everything that can go wrong with a relationship and it's natural to want to try and protect your child from bad experiences. What's important is to keep in mind that there are good people out there just waiting to be asked to be part of your child's life. Your child is going to need them, because you won't be able to protect your child forever.

When people know the potential for harm in relationships and they choose to try anyway, they are exercising the "right to risk." I can't think of a better way to describe what's lost by people with disabilities when they are sheltered away from society than with the poem on the next page, offered by the organization "Parent Advocacy."

THE DIGNITY OF RISK

What if you never got to make a mistake.

What if your money was always kept in an envelope where you couldn't get it.

What if you were never given a chance to do well at something.

What if your only chance to be with people different from you was with your own family.

What if the job you did was not useful.

What if you never got to make a decision.

What if the only risky thing you could do was act out.

What if you couldn't go outside because the last time you went it rained.

What if you took the wrong bus once and now you can't take another one.

What if you got into trouble and were sent away and you couldn't come back because they always remember your "trouble."

What if you worked and got paid $.46 an hour.

What if you had to wear your winter coat when it rained because it was all you had.

What if you had no privacy.

What if you could do part of the grocery shopping but weren't allowed because you couldn't do all of the shopping.

What if you spent three hours every day just waiting.

What if you grew old and never knew adulthood.

What if you never got a chance.

CHAPTER 8

HOW HAVE OTHERS INCORPORATED THESE IDEAS?

S ometimes it is difficult to imagine how all of these contacts and ideas will mesh with your child's life. Will the changes be unwieldy and awkward? What if you can't manage everything at once? Is a little bit of change okay?

I have included four stories to illustrate how different people moved toward building larger social networks. As you will see, they all have different types of disabilities and levels of functioning, as well as different concepts of what constitutes success. See if you can identify some of the common denominators in their stories.

JONATHAN

Jonathan was born intellectually gifted. One day when he was ten, he and his younger brother were racing on their bikes. The attractive blond, blue-eyed boy neglected to stop for a stop sign. Jonathan rode into the path of a green Buick, smashing his head through the windshield. The driver was overcome with remorse; he said he never saw Jonathan until it was too late.

Jonathan spent about a month in a coma. Specialists removed about a quarter of his brain. When he finally regained consciousness, he had lost the ability to speak and to move the right side of his body. He had also lost his ability to learn things quickly, and, since he was under the age of twenty-one when the accident occurred, he joined the ranks of people with developmental disabilities.

Jonathan's mother had been treated for depression in the past. The stress of the accident increased her vulnerability to mental illness. She became very ill and was hospitalized. Jonathan's father left his mother, fought for custody of Jonathan and his younger brother, Timothy, and won.

A few years later, Jonathan's father felt he could no longer deal with his two children and abandoned them to their grandmother. He sent support checks from time to time. Visits decreased, eventually becoming almost non-existent.

Grandmom felt up to the challenge of raising Jonathan. By this time, he was starting to walk again, though he had a terrible gait. Grandmom vehemently refused to put him in a home, as was suggested to her several times. "He's doing great!" she would shout. "He's doing just fine!"

Grandmom fought with the Buick driver's insurance company and won. It took more than eight years, but she obtained a sizeable settlement for Jonathan, including coverage for all his medical bills.

She hired tutors for him to work on his speech. She decided to enroll him in karate class to improve his gait. Jonathan improved by leaps and bounds, much to everyone's surprise—everyone's surprise, except Grandmom's. "I told you so!" she would say, wagging her finger. "My Jonathan's doing just great!"

She insisted that he go to the neighborhood high school. He was in a special class part of the day, but did well with high school math. He got a job where Grandmom shopped, working part time in the bakery.

Against many people's objections, she got him driving lessons and a car. He had some accidents, minor fender benders, but Grandmom was undaunted. "Of course, he can drive!"

After high school, Jonathan went on to community college. It didn't work out. Jonathan couldn't keep his grades up, even with private tutors. "So what?" Grandmom shrugged. He got involved in a bowling league (for nondisabled people). Jonathan wasn't the best bowler they had ever seen, but he wasn't the worst, either. He made a couple of friends in the league, and they started to pal around together. They spend a lot of time talking about how to meet women.

Eventually Grandmom noticed that Jonathan loved children, and they loved him. He could always make them laugh. He was very considerate of them and listened to them attentively. She decided that Jonathan had some kind of future working with children. They tried baby sitting, looked into day care—nothing seemed to fit.

One day, Grandmom hit on clowning. "We'll be Sonny and Honey! We'll go all over and clown! We'll make animal balloons! We'll do magic tricks! We'll make $50 an hour!" Jonathan was interested. Jonathan's uncle, a human service professional and Grandmom's son, thought it was a terrible idea.

"No! Don't make him out to be a clown! People already think of people with disabilities as clowns! Don't put him in that position. Don't perpetuate the stereotype!"

"Nonsense," shouted Grandmom (she always shouts). "Jonathan's going to do just great!"

So they went to clown college. They got clown diplomas. Now they go to birthday parties and entertain children. Magic tricks, animal balloons, and, yes, $50 an hour. Each.

Jonathan now has a wide network of friends (other clowns), and he earns good money doing something that he loves. He's seen as a valuable asset because of his gift of working with children and is frequently called upon to help other clowns with their jobs. Grandmom knows that Jonathan will be devastated when she dies, but she feels that he has enough friends and contacts to help him out of any jam in which he may find himself.

Samantha

Samantha was born with Down syndrome. Her mother, Beverly, was completely taken by surprise. She was shocked. How could this happen? Beverly's family was also shocked. They didn't even visit her in the hospital.

Then Beverly got a call from another mom of a child with Down syndrome. The other mom gave her good advice, told her about a parent support group in the area, and dropped off some books for her to read. The other mom congratulated her on Samantha's birth. She was the only person who did.

That was eight years ago.

Beverly is a fast learner. Today, she's vice president of a parent advocacy organization. She knows a lot about federal legislation and how it affects her child. She has made friends with a state legislator who lives nearby. He knows Samantha and Beverly well. Together, they work on problems with the state system.

Beverly tries to educate other people about Down syndrome whenever she can. When she thinks about the way people reacted to Samantha's birth, she gets very, very angry. Beverly tries hard to make sure that other mothers aren't treated the same way.

Samantha has inherited her mother's fiery spirit. She's a superb athlete, playing Little League baseball with nondisabled children. Despite her strong athletic ability, however, the team didn't want to accept her because of her disability. Beverly took care of that problem in about two minutes flat. She called the Little League organizer and educated him about the Americans with Disabilities Act and the Office of Civil Rights complaint procedures. The Little League organizer wisely decided to allow Samantha to participate.

Samantha is known for her "take no prisoners" style of play. She's a very pretty little girl with long brown hair which she ties up into a pony tail for the game. One day, I saw her steal second base on a signal from the coach. The opposing baseman, annoyed at her success, stood on the base right beside her. Samantha didn't like that and repeatedly shoved him off. The second baseman got more annoyed. Samantha's dad shouted encouragement.

"Hang in there, Sammy! Don't let him intimidate you!"

As if he could.

Samantha takes ballet with one of her sisters, and swims at the YMCA. Beverly is a devout Catholic and wanted all of her children to benefit from religious education. There was some concern about whether Samantha could participate with all the other little children. Beverly took care of that problem too. Again, she went to her priest and explained the law. The priest knew Beverly well enough to sense that she wouldn't back down, and like the Little League organizer, allowed Samantha to be included.

Once Samantha was given a chance, she became a valued participant in Little League and in her religious education classes. She was liked for her own strong personality, and even had a boyfriend before long. Beverly's aggressiveness forced adults to deal with her daughter despite their prejudices. When they actually came face to face with Samantha, they realized that they could accommodate her special needs. This opened doors for other kids with disabilities.

This year, Samantha will be fully included in a regular education classroom for the first time. Beverly's scared to death. She's worried that Samantha will get picked on by the other kids, that she'll lose her self-confidence.

Samantha's dad isn't concerned a bit.

MIKE AND LOUISE

Mike and Louise used to live in a state-operated institution. They knew each other for years, gradually falling in love. Mike is the more articulate of the two. Louise is more in touch with her feelings. They both carry labels of mental retardation.

After about twenty years, there was a lawsuit that forced the state to close the institution. The process took several years. Mike was one of the first to move out, while Louise had to stay behind. Louise was identified as "difficult to place" because she was a "behavior problem."

Mike moved into a group home and joined a new self-advocacy group for people with disabilities. He quickly became a leader and a spokesperson. He was celebrated for his ability to "tell it like it is." He put pressure on legislators and advocates to close all institutions for people with mental retardation. In the meanwhile, he maintained contact with Louise, still living in the institution. They missed each other terribly.

Finally, Louise moved into a group home for eight women. She was unhappy with her living arrangement, however, and continued to have problems with behavior.

Mike asked her to marry him. Louise accepted. Mike then turned his advocacy skills to good use, pushing for an apartment for him and Louise alone. Eventually, Mike won. They married and moved in together, paying for the apartment and staff with government assistance.

Louise's behavior problems have all but disappeared. She still gets emotional sometimes, but Mike is right there, rubbing her back, whispering to her to calm down. She listens and calms. They have the right to hire and fire the support staff who assist them with things on a weekly basis. They talk about buying a house, but they don't know how to make it work financially. Mike still does a lot of advocacy, and he takes Louise with him. She's also a person of strong conviction, not afraid to speak her mind. Other than being overwhelmed by the problems they face in their advocacy, they appear to be a contented couple.

MATTHEW

Matthew lives with his mother and father, the youngest of four sons. He is in his mid-twenties. His parents have always felt it important to include Matthew in every aspect of their lives. Matthew is well-known in his neighborhood, spending time outside sitting in his wheelchair, soaking up some sun.

Matthew is labeled with profound mental retardation and cerebral palsy. He has a serious seizure condition that regularly threatens his life. He has a very wobbly gait and uses a wheelchair most of the time. He doesn't speak. A communication device was tried once, but Matthew didn't seem to like it.

Matthew's parents are relatively young and in good health. They don't expect Matthew to outlive them. Even so, they have made arrangements for a friend to assume guardianship of him should they both pass away. If this happens, their friend wants Matthew to move into his home, but would need the government to provide support staff to help care for Matthew. Matthew's parents are advocating with the government to make more of these in-home supports possible. (See Chapter 10 for more information.) They recognize that as they get older, they're also going to need some assistance to maintain him in the family home.

In the meantime, Matthew enjoys all the richness of a large family. If his parents have to go out of town, he often stays with one of his brothers. Occasionally, if he's healthy, he travels with his parents. There is a woman who is hired to stay with him while his mom is at work. She's from down the street and has known Matthew for about ten years. His parents drive him to a day program for pre-vocational training a couple of times a week. They want him to have more nondisabled friends, but have had to concentrate more on keeping him physically well. He's had some very serious problems in the last year, and has landed in the hospital on several occasions. Once he nearly died.

Matthew had a high school graduation party two years ago. More than forty people came. Most were members of his extended family, but neighbors came too. It was a great day with lots of sunshine and people of all ages milling around. Matthew sat in the middle of it all, soaking up the sun.

WHAT IS SUCCESS?

Success means different things to different people. Some people with disabilities have huge networks of nondisabled friends. Others don't. Matthew's vision of success is going to look very different from Samantha's. Your child's will be unique as well.

I think it's important to note here that developing social networks is a process. It's a lifelong effort. All of the families in the examples above are constantly pushing for just a little bit more each day. For Jonathan, that may mean a full-time job. For Matthew, it may mean inviting someone over to the house more often.

The individuals profiled above fail occasionally, but that doesn't stand in their way. Jonathan had a lot of difficulty in college, so he had to change some of his career goals. Matthew still gets a lot of stares when he goes out. It's a little uncomfortable, but everyone seems to take the staring in stride.

Each of the stories demonstrates that community contacts are paying off. Twenty years ago, it was unheard of for a kid with Down syndrome to go to a regular third grade class. Samantha has more opportunities today, precisely because she is so well networked. Each of the people described above is also paving the way for others with disabilities. The legislator is going to expect to have people with disabilities in his hometown, the baker may be more open-minded when choosing employees, and the restaurant owners in Matthew's hometown will know a lot about serving people in wheelchairs.

All of these families also work hard to keep up with issues facing people with disabilities. Mike maintains contact with his self-advocacy group; Beverly continually learns through her parent organization. Jonathan's grandmother is always checking in with his uncle, a professional advocate.

Keeping up with this kind of information can help reveal new opportunities for people with disabilities. Many new services are first offered through "pilot programs," or demonstration grants. Well-educated advocates are often the first to hear about such programs, and some of the first in line to take advantage of the new service. This information is pretty easy to obtain. See Chapter 12 for more information on how you can get involved.

It's important to recognize that these aren't fanciful stories. Nobody's living happily ever after. Jonathan desperately wants a girlfriend, and Samantha's probably going to have to do a better job managing her temper this year. Mike and Louise are constantly besieged by requests for assistance by people who want to move out of institutions. Matthew may not live another year.

While they could all point out imperfections in their lifestyles, I don't think any of them would want to move off to some isolated program somewhere. I know that they wouldn't give up their family and friends. Not for a minute.

I offer these stories of success to illustrate two major points. First, you and your child are going to have a highly individualized vision of what you want the future to look like. (Refer back to Chapters Two and Four for guidance in developing a vision for your child.) Second, you need to work toward that vision constantly. Don't give up. Once your child has a strong network, you can take the next step of identifying one or more people who are willing to make a long-term commitment to your child.

CHAPTER 9

How Do I Ask
Someone to Make a
Long-Term Commitment
to My Child?

Helping your child expand her network of friends can be extremely hard work. But there are valuable payoffs when you succeed. First, your child can enjoy all the same benefits of having a rich and varied life that everybody else does. She will feel loved and accepted, enjoy outside activities with a favorite companion, and be appreciated for her own self. And second, your child may encounter someone who would like to make a lifetime commitment to help her.

In making plans for your child's future without you, it is important to be honest with yourself about the types of assistance she will need. You don't want to sell your child short and limit her independence, but you also don't want to overestimate her abilities and fail to provide for important needs. Some adults with disabilities need only intermittent support to live on their own. For example, they may need somebody to act as a sounding board or a system-wise advocate, or to help them file their annual tax return if they are employed. Others need more assistance on a regular basis. They may need someone to speak up for them at program planning meetings, or someone to take complete control of any funds left by their parents for their use, or someone to accompany them to regular medical or psychological appointments. Still others need even more intensive support, such as assistance with dressing, bathing, and making meals, daily assistance with transportation, or frequent visits to make sure they are happy and safe.

If you completed the Support Checklist in Chapter 2, you should have a good idea of the amount and types of practical support your child will need after your death. At this point, it may also help if you think about all the large and small things you do for her just to try to make her happy. Do you call her every evening so you can find out how her day went and boost her spirits if necessary? Do you always watch a certain TV show together and chuckle at the silly jokes? Do you buy the latest issue of her favorite comic book for her as soon as it hits the stand? How important is it to you and your child that someone continue to do these types of things for her when you are gone?

Whatever kinds of practical or emotional support your child may need, *someone* is going to have to provide it. Earlier chapters of this book dealt with bringing your child into contact with people who might eventually be interested in making a responsible, lifetime commitment to support her. This chapter explains how to identify one or more individuals who could assist your child and how to ask them whether they will look out for your child after your death.

Setting the Stage

Compare your Support Checklist results with the abilities of your child's current friends. Are there any matches? For example, is there someone obvious like a bookkeeper who can help with your child's checkbook? A short order cook who can help with menu planning? A good friend who seems like a long-term source of advice? If so, spend some time getting to know more about those people. Talk openly about your concerns for your child's future a few times before asking for a commitment. Chances are the friend is concerned too.

Sometimes, it may not seem feasible to find a single person who will take on complete responsibility for your child's future well-being. It may be easier for someone to make a long-term commitment to your child if he or she has the support of a circle of friends. A circle of friends is a group of people who come together periodically to assist and support an individual with different issues such as finding a job, moving to a new place, expanding social contacts, etc. Members agree to fulfill different roles and responsibilities. One benefit of this approach is that if one friend moves away or can't continue her involvement for some other reason, another member of the group can pick up the slack.

If you are considering having many different people provide support (a good idea!), consider organizing them into a circle of friends. If you have only identified two people to support your child, but need four more, go ahead and ask for their commitments anyway if the timing seems right. Often, someone will come into a circle of friends expecting to provide one type of support and actually do something else. In any event, the circle of friends or the single advocate will probably be called upon to recruit others to assist with unexpected problems or events in the future.

EVALUATING YOUR CHOICE

Sometimes it will take awhile for you to identify one or more likely candidates to make a commitment to your child. You will want to make sure that their relationship with your child is a lasting thing, not a fad or whim. You may also want to make sure that they are capable of guiding your child's affairs. Depending on your child's abilities, this can take time. Sometimes you are not going to be able to glean all the information you need to know about someone from casual contact. You may need to sit down with the person, tell them about your interest in having them involved with your child after your death, and ask them what you need to know. Here are some general questions to consider:

- Does the friend get along with my son/daughter?
- Does the friend give good advice without negating what my son/daughter wants to do?
- Does my son/daughter trust, like, and feel comfortable with the person?
- Does the friend seem able to handle money?
- Is the friend capable of sticking with my child for the long term? (This will probably take months to determine.) Does he or she have other long-term relationships in his or her life?
- Do our feelings about what my son/daughter needs agree?
- Will the person see that my last wishes are carried out?
- Is the friend interested in taking on such a life-long responsibility?
- Is the person likely to stay in the same geographical area? If not, can he or she provide the type of support needed from a distance?

If the answers to the above questions are yes, wonderful! You've found someone who may be interested in looking out for your child after your death. Even if most of the answers are yes and some are no, you may still have a very strong candidate. For example, some friends may fail the money test. The woman loves your daughter, your daughter raves about her friend, you and the woman see eye to eye on a lot of issues, but she's terrible with money. This doesn't mean she needs to be ruled out. You could try to set up a trust fund which is very explicit (see your attorney, preferably one who is knowledgeable about disabilities and estate planning, for suggestions on this), or you could ask someone else to act as a trust officer or guardian on financial issues. Or you may want to consider that many people are terrible with their own money, but for some reason, highly responsible with someone else's funds.

Some people worry about the age of the people in your child's support network. Ideally, you might want to choose someone younger than you are, but don't make this an iron-clad rule. It's more important to find someone who is caring and responsible.

TAKING THE PLUNGE

Once you know who you are going to ask to do what, the next step is to arrange a meeting. Try to hold the meeting in a place where you will both feel comfortable and can talk without worrying about interruptions and time constraints.

Here are some points to cover when asking someone to make a long-term, and hopefully life-long, commitment to your child:

- **An explanation of your child's vulnerability -** This could include a discussion about her inability to manage finances, problems with sexuality, etc.
- **Reasons that paid professionals may not be able to fill the role -** for example, conflicts with work responsibilities, turnover, etc.
- **Explain what role, if any, other family members will play, and why you still feel that you need other assistance**
- **Your hopes for your child's life**
- **Your fears**
- **Why this person would be a good advocate** (i.e. because of his or her respect for your child, or because he or she would not be intimidated by human service professionals, or because of his or her positive approach to solving problems, etc.)
- **What you would like him or her to do -** have your child move in, visit her weekly at a group home, manage her finances, attend program meetings, take her to church, etc.
- **Mention other people who may already have committed to help.** Explain how this person fits in and whether he or she should coordinate information or efforts.

- **A concrete request for long-term assistance:** "Would you be willing to be a life-long advocate for my child?" (or be her trust officer, balance her checkbook every month, etc.)

- **Also explain what you're *not* asking them to do.** In particular, explain that you're not asking them to take over responsibility for paying for everything your child needs. Some people may worry about this possiblity—that by agreeing to look out for your child they would become liable for all her expenses. Try to anticipate such concerns and reassure the person in advance.

- **A plea not to walk away if your child is placed in some kind of residential situation.** This may be the time when a friend is needed most.

Here's how some other parents have gone about asking someone to make a long-term commitment to their children:

Janice and Tom invited their daughter's friend, Naomi, over for a cup of coffee. Their daughter, Kimberly, talks non-stop about Naomi, even though they have been friends for over two years. Janice took the lead in getting the two together. Her contact with Naomi had been frequent in the beginning of the relationship, but as Naomi and Kimberly got to know each other, Janice's involvement decreased.

Janice and Tom identified Naomi as someone who would be ideal to be involved with their daughter after their deaths. Naomi and Kimberly were very close, and Kimberly often shared things with Naomi that she didn't even tell her mother. In addition, Naomi was always sensitive to Kimberly's needs and feelings but never seemed to pity her. Janice noticed that Kimberly seemed to develop more self-assurance as her relationship with Naomi progressed.

Janice opened the subject by talking about her own fears for Kimberly after she and her husband die, stressing the need for someone in Kimberly's life to advocate on her behalf. Janice went on to explain how social workers are sometimes good advocates, but that they are conflicted because of their paid status and job pressures. Tom talked about his concern that Kimberly could wind up in an unhappy living situation, away from her neighborhood and friends who have sustained her for most of her thirty-two years.

Janice and Tom had it easy. At this point, Naomi was gripped with fear for her friend. She said that she had never realized that people with cognitive disabilities were so vulnerable. She asked what she could do to help out.

Janice outlined her ideas for Kimberly's life. She said they wanted Kimberly to live with one or two other people around her own age whom she liked and got on with. They wanted Naomi to do whatever she could do to see that that's what happened. They wanted Naomi to maintain her friendship with Kimberly, making sure that Kimberly was all right, and to act as Kimberly's advocate, participating in program planning meetings, interceding with land-lords, whatever. Tom added that they also wanted Naomi to oversee Kimberly's trust fund, making sure that the money was used properly and in accor-dance with Janice's and Tom's wishes.

Naomi said she was flattered and that it sounded like something she might like to do, but she wanted to discuss it with her husband first. Naomi went home, and Janice and Tom waited on pins and needles to hear her response.

Naomi called back the next day, saying that her husband thought it was something that needed to be done and she would be happy to be involved with Kimberly for the long term. Janice and Tom were delighted and Janice scheduled some time to talk more with Naomi about her new role.

❖

Harris, Thomas's father, took a slightly different approach. He and Thomas had talked about friends who might be good "helpers" after he wasn't able to go to Thomas's meetings anymore. Thomas had an unsuccessful experience with a private institution when he was young and was well aware of the problems he could encounter in such places. He often said to his dad, with whom he was now living, "I don't want to go back there." Thomas was very keen on the idea that he might need some assistance to live the way he wanted after his father passed away.

Harris and Thomas picked three friends who might be able to act in the capacity needed. They took all three friends out to dinner at the nicest restaurant in town and Harris simply said, "We need someone to look out for Thomas after I'm not around anymore. We wanted to know if any of you would be interested?"

One friend said he was, but wanted to know more about what was required. By the end of the discussion, all three friends said that they would do what was needed.

Unfortunately, one friend discontinued his relationship with Thomas a short time later. He suddenly wasn't available to play basketball anymore, complaining that his job was too demanding. Eventually, the relationship ended. Harris feels that this friend probably was uncomfortable with the commitment he had made and looked for a way out. Thomas still has two other friends who want to maintain their relationship as long as they can. Harris and Thomas are looking for even more people who may be interested in such a commitment. Their view, "the more the merrier."

❖

Kay took the approach of building a "circle of friends" around her son, Steve. Kay originally put the group together to help Steve find a job. She asked her sister, Steve's aunt, to be involved, along with some friends of Steve's. Kay also recruited a human services worker who knew Steve and got along with him. By the time she was ready, she had eight people who agreed to support Steve in his efforts to find a job.

One night, while the group was eating pizza and working on Steve's job situation, Kay told them how worried she was about Steve's future. She said that he was likely to need support like this for different issues after she passed away, and she was concerned that no one would care enough about him to organize support circles like this one. Kay added that she had an image of him, lonely and abused, with no one around who cared.

People were stunned. After a few minutes of silence, one woman said that she would be willing to keep meeting about Steve even after he got a job if that would help. Other members of the group agreed.

Kay then told her son's friends how vital they were to Steve's life and emphasized that she wanted them to be involved with him after her death. This was a wise move. Americans are very private people and won't often involve themselves in someone else's life. Kay's invitation gave these people the permission they needed to be Steve's lifelong advocates.

The group now sees its responsibility as a long-term commitment. They have begun to toss around ideas about where Steve might live after his mother's death and to gently question Kay about her plans to manage her estate.

WHEN THE ANSWER IS "YES"

Let's say you got a positive response. Congratulations! Now what? After thanking the person, like Janice and Tom did with Naomi, you will probably want to schedule another time to begin sharing information about your child's needs and desires. You may even want to start bringing the person to your child's program planning meetings or to meet her casemanager. These steps can be taken gradually over time or done right away—whichever way you feel the most comfortable. Some families meet with the person and explain their will, for example. Other families just let things go until the person steps in upon the parents' death, though a gradual, parent-supported transition would be best for everyone. As Chapter 11 explains, there are many good reasons to implement your plan before you die.

You will probably want to develop some kind of written document detailing all the important things the person or persons will need to know after you die, including:

- What financial arrangements have been made to provide for your child's needs
- The name and phone number of the family attorney
- Where important documents are and who has access to them
- Names and phone numbers of important people in your child's life, including everyone who will be helping to look after her and who has agreed to do what
- Your child's eligibility for various government programs
- Where your child is supposed to live, if she has been living with parents
- IEP, IHP, what programs she's on the waiting list for, casemanager's name and phone number
- Medical information, names of doctors, dentists, etc.
- Anything else that seems appropriate.

WHEN THE ANSWER IS "NO"

Unfortunately, you may strike out the first (or even second or third time) you ask someone to make a lifelong commitment to your child. A "no" response is obviously much harder to deal with, as the story below illustrates:

Darcell took Natalie out to lunch and they talked warmly about Jackie, Darcell's daughter. Natalie said how much she enjoyed their time together and Darcell felt the time was right to ask the big question.

She covered all the important issues: her fears for Jackie, the need for non-paid people in her daughter's life, etc. Darcell wound up with the request, "Will you be my daughter's advocate after I die?"

Natalie's reaction was immediately negative. She didn't feel that she could make a lifelong commitment to anyone. She reiterated that she really liked Jackie, but she thought Darcell should look for someone else.

Darcell was crushed. She had been so sure that Natalie was the perfect choice. Perhaps she had asked too much of Natalie too soon, but she was disappointed nonetheless. She murmured that she understood Natalie's objections and said that she would look for someone else. The lunch ended on an uncomfortable note.

A few days later, Darcell called Natalie and invited her over to the house to have dinner and work on some craft projects with Jackie. Darcell went to some pains to make Natalie's favorite meal. Despite her efforts, the atmosphere was still tense.

Finally, Darcell took Natalie aside and said, "I'm afraid that our talk the other day may have made you uncomfortable. I asked you because you are such an important part of Jackie's life. She really looks forward to your visits and I would hate to have anything I did ruin that for either of you. I appreciated your honesty and regret that I may have put you in a tough spot."

Natalie got teary eyed and said that she felt guilty turning down Darcell's request. She reiterated that she really loved Jackie and didn't want to see anything happen to her, but she felt it was dishonest to promise something that she couldn't be sure she could deliver. The two hugged and Jackie ended up keeping her friend.

In the wake of her discussions with Natalie, Darcell realized that she had stopped worrying about expanding Jackie's social network once she identified Natalie as a possible advocate. She began all over again, this time using Natalie as a resource person to help introduce Jackie to others.

It's hard to say how you might feel when you get a negative response. Some parents don't see why anyone would want to take on such a responsibility in the first place. Consequently, they have more trouble dealing with a "yes" than a "no." Other parents feel personal rejection and anger that they've been turned down. In these cases, it's important to recognize that the rejection was probably not a reflection on you or your child—it was the person's inability to make the long-term commitment. Just as with any major disappointment, you need to focus on what has been going well and try again with someone else. You may even want to try later with the same person. Darcell was able to work through her disappointment and focus on what mattered most; Natalie is still important to Jackie and needs to be a part of her life. She immediately worked to repair any damage that may have occurred and started to look for other options.

I once asked another human service worker how she maintained her high spirits even though she was having difficulty finding non-paid companions for people living in a group home. She responded that she had adopted a guiding principle that there are good people in the world who are more than willing to befriend people with disabilities. I've found this to be true and you will too. You just have to believe that there are people out there who would love to be involved with your child. If you look in the right places, you will find them.

CHAPTER **10**

What Have Other People Done in My Situation?

E ven if many people have committed to supporting your child after your death, you may still need to investigate residential programs for him. No one in your support group may have the room for your child to move in with them, or your son may just want to move away from home. If you think your child may need to find another place to live after you or your spouse dies, it may be wise to look into making that move now. Usually it is easier if the parents make housing or financial arrangements for their child before they die. In addition, a parent's death can be very traumatic, and it would be better not to compound the stress with a sudden move.

This chapter includes information on different types of residential and financial arrangements for individuals with disabilities. You can use the list to help identify what *may* be available in your own community, but you will have to investigate to discover which options are actually offered in your area. Unfortunately, not all options are available everywhere.

RESIDENTIAL OPTIONS

"I'm not sure what is available to my son. What kinds of options does he have for a living situation? It's hard to imagine what he might like best if we don't know what's out there."

There are many different types of residential arrangements for adults with disabilities. You should be forewarned, however, that there are often long waiting lists for good programs. Most states have waiting lists that cannot be filled for years—if ever. This means that it is advisable to start looking at your options early. By the same token, if you need to create a new program, it's important to find that out as soon as possible.

You can start by getting a list of the residential options in your community from your local human services branch of the government. Often this will be called the Office or Department of Mental Retardation or Developmental Disabilities. Find out what the eligibility criteria are for these programs and make sure your child qualifies before you begin your search. Eligibility criteria vary from state to state and program to program. Most often to qualify, a person must have functioning below a certain level, a particular type of diagnosis (such as mental retardation), and financial need. Qualifying may mean that you can get financial or rehabilitative assistance. If your child does not qualify, you may be able to appeal the decision or apply to another government agency. If you find that no government agency will pay for the cost of your child's care, you can always arrange to pay privately. For residential care, however, this is often expensive.

Once you have a list of programs that your child qualifies for, arrange to visit them. Any reputable provider will be proud to show you their services. Take your family, including your son or daughter with the disability, ask any questions you can think of, and collect all the written material they're willing to give you. Pay particular attention to the way you feel when you are in the facility. Is this a place where you would like to live? If not, chances are your child wouldn't, either.

Ultimately, the program you choose should depend on your family member's needs, available government funding, ability to pay, and his lifestyle wishes. Some basic factors that you may want to consider include:

Staff

- How much assistance does your son need? Twenty-four-hour care, thirty hours a week? Less?
- What is the staff-to-resident ratio?
- Who hires staff? Would your child be involved in the selection process?
- Does he need staff with special expertise, such as occupational therapists, physical therapists, etc.?

Community Access

- Is frequent access to community activities encouraged?
- What activities are there? Can these be modified to suit the desire of your child?
- How close will he live to shopping centers and recreational sites? Can he walk to them? Is there a bus available? How will he get around?

Relations with the Opposite Sex

- What is the program's attitudes toward dating, sex, and marriage?

Home Ownership

- Who owns the home, your child or the provider, or is it rented?

Transportation

- If your child wants to go to different events, how is that arranged?

Daily Living Activities
- Who maintains the home, cooks the food, does the shopping?

Growth Opportunities
- Are there opportunities to improve skills, become more independent, learn new things?

Consumer Control
- How much control will your child be able to exercise over his own life? Will he plan his own day? His meals? Decide what to wear?
- Will he choose furnishings and decorative items for his home?
- Can he go to bed when he wants?
- Can he control the TV remote?
- Is there unrestricted access to family and friends? What about the telephone?
- How does the program encourage consumer choice and control?
- What if he has a complaint? What happens?

Another important consideration is how your death and that of your spouse is likely to affect your child's placement in a particular program. If your child is an adult and his program is being paid for by the government, his placement should be unaffected if you or your spouse dies. This doesn't mean that the arrangement is permanent, however. The government always has the option of moving people around, and the provider agency could go out of business. If your child is under the age of majority in your state (usually 21), placement could be negatively affected by the parents' death. Sometimes, facilities are paid through the state's department of education, which usually fund only until the age of twenty-one. Still other facilities may opt only to serve children, no matter who provides the funding. Check with your government agency to determine what would happen to your child.

Supported Living

The term "supported living" refers to people with cognitive disabilities living in their own home and receiving only as much support as necessary to lead a happy life. Support can vary in intensity from weekly visits to a live-in staff member, though some states limit the amount of support that can be provided for this kind of care (for example, thirty hours or less per week).

In one successful supported living arrangement, two women with mental retardation live in an apartment in Philadelphia. They have an agreement with a local social service agency to assist them with essential daily living tasks, such as banking. They also meet with a social worker regularly to discuss any problems that may have come up and to make additional requests for assistance. The best part of the arrangement is that the women get to hire and fire their support staff. They participated in interviews with the agency director and selected a person everyone agreed upon. The social worker knows that if he fails to meet their needs they may ask him to leave. This arrangement makes the women feel empowered to express their needs and reminds the social worker who he's supposed to be working for. Not all supported living arrangements allow such involvement in the selection of staff but it seems to be a trend for the future. The cost of renting the residence and support staff is usually funded by the state government or a combination of state and federal funds, unless the resident can afford to pay.

In Home Supports

A new trend in residential care is to offer "in home supports." This means that assistance is given to the family to maintain the person in his or her own home, usually with other family members (parents, siblings, etc.). This type of support can range from a personal assistant for the person with the disability to help with bathing, getting to work, etc., to a licensed nurse to provide assistance for those with serious medical conditions (home health care), to monthly respite care for the family. I have heard of some highly individualized types of in home supports, including the provision of staff to assist with behavior problems during the person's waking hours and the purchase of a small transportable respirator that enabled an infant with breathing problems to live at home. With such support, someone who was previously overwhelmed by the idea may be able to take your child into their own home.

Foster Care

This term refers to an arrangement in which a person with mental retardation lives with a foster family in the foster family's own home. Foster families are recruited and screened by government or private agencies and receive a government subsidy to cover the cost of care. Sometimes, foster families are given some basic training on proper care and nutrition. A major drawback of this type of arrangement is that it is frequently designed as a temporary situation. It is often intended to give someone training so that they can become more independent and live on their own.

Sometimes, foster care arrangements do become permanent by mutual agreement. The amount of time that someone would live with one family can vary. Check the program's guidelines and ask questions about average length of stay when you investigate this option. One very positive aspect of foster care is that it is in a very natural family setting, probably quite similar to the home where the person with mental retardation used to live.

Family Living

This is similar to a foster care arrangement in certain respects— namely, a natural family receives a subsidy from the government to care for an adult or child with mental retardation in their own home. One difference is that the host families may receive better, more specialized training and support services to assist in the care of the person. Careful attention is usually paid to matching the individual with disabilities to the family, so there are often plenty of opportunities to meet the host family and to get to know them. It is also hoped that the arrangement will be permanent, though either party can opt out if they wish. Host families usually make use of camps and day programs to provide respite, just like natural families do.

Group Homes, Large and Small

This is the type of residential program that most parents seem to be familiar with. Typically set in the community, right next to "normal" homes, group homes allow access to shopping, neighbors, and other community resources. Group homes are often divided into two types— small and large. Large bed group facilities house over fifteen people, while small group homes house fifteen and under. The trend here is toward much smaller facilities, with preferences for three, two, or even one resident. The government usually pays for placement in a group home, though some parents pay for placements themselves.

Group homes often have twenty-four-hour staffing. The staff are usually high school graduates at a minimum, with more experienced supervisors off-site. Staff may or may not live in the group home. There is usually a daily schedule of activities which is designed to assist the residents in learning various skills, such as housekeeping.

Some group homes have strict eligibility guidelines. For example, some group homes have rules that say that if your child is doing well enough to hold down a job, he's not disabled enough to live at that particular group home. Some places cater to people with medical needs or behavioral problems. Specialized facilities will usually be identified up front.

Some group homes are better at encouraging consumer control and choice than others. Beware of group homes that are very isolated and don't have much contact with the outside world. Professionals refer to such group homes as "mini institutions," meaning that they really offer no advantage over institutional living, because they provide little access to the community.

Clustered Apartment Programs

The term "clustered apartment settings" refers to a group of apartments located in one apartment complex that are all rented out by the same social service agency. One apartment is given to support staff, who are on call to residents, or consumers, living in other apartments. In addition, staff provide a varying number of hours of support and education each week. This may take the form of working on cooking skills, transporting people to doctor's appointments, etc. Usually two, but sometimes three, adults live in each apartment. Consumers are responsible for their own housekeeping, but may have assistance from staff. The apartment rent is usually covered by the provider agency for both consumers and staff. Many times consumers are required to contribute to the rent using Social Security or Supplemental Security Income checks.

Some clustered apartment programs function as "independent training programs," meaning that they are temporary and the person with the disability is expected to move out on his own at graduation. For instance, there are two-year programs which offer group classes on budgeting and cooking.

Semi-Independent Living

In other forms of semi-independent living, an adult with disabilities may live alone or with roommates in an apartment or a house, with staff living nearby, but not in the same dwelling. Staff usually provide support as needed on housekeeping, cooking, budgeting, relationships, etc. Residents may pay for their home themselves or receive some type of government assistance. Support staff often serve several residents, but the number depends on how much support and time each person needs.

Boarding Homes

This is an option that provides a room with a bed and sometimes one hot meal. Typically, little to no supervision is provided, just as in any boarding house. The resident is usually responsible for his room rent. If your son or daughter requires virtually no supervision, this can be a great, low-cost option. Unfortunately, there have been a lot of complaints about poor boarding home care and managers taking advantage of people with cognitive disabilities. If you decide to choose a boarding home, make your selection carefully.

Personal Care Facility

A personal care facility provides staff to attend to a person's physical needs such as bathing, cooking, dressing, etc., but does not provide any formal training. This is in contrast to a group home, which usually places a lot of emphasis on teaching people to become more independent. Personal care facilities are usually more "custodial" in nature and may not provide staff assistance twenty-four hours a day. Personal care facilities can be funded privately or with government subsidies.

Board and Supervision Facility

This is a program that provides a place to sleep, meals, and basic supervision. In contrast to group homes and personal care facilities, there is no formal training or assistance with daily living skills such as dressing and bathing. These facilities also differ from nursing homes in that they do not offer medical care. Board and supervision facilities can be funded privately or with government subsidies.

Private Institutions

A private institution is a large facility, often specializing in serving people with cognitive disabilities. It usually consists of several large buildings and sometimes, smaller cottages, set in a campus-style arrangement. Staff are usually high school graduates, providing 24-hour coverage, with more qualified personnel supervising. Institutions usually provide some kind of training in daily living skills, work skills, etc. There are usually at least sixteen residents in such a setting, and some facilities house hundreds of residents. Most activities take place on the campus and vary greatly from facility to facility. Some private institutions take people into the community to go shopping, to church, etc. Fees for staying in a private institution can be paid by the government or by the family.

Public Institutions

A public institution is a large facility, usually consisting of several large buildings set in a campus-style arrangement out in the country somewhere. It is similar to a private institution in design except that it is funded and operated by the government, instead of by a private agency.

Some parents are pleased with the care their children receive in such facilities, but there is a trend against such settings. Some states have gone as far as closing all their public institutions, moving residents into smaller community-based homes. Other states have plans to do the same thing. In fact, all but one state, Nevada, have reduced their public institution population in the last ten years. The arguments against public institutions are numerous, but mainly, people feel that people with mental retardation deserve the right to live in the community like the rest of us.

The objections to institutions go beyond concerns about community inclusion. Taxpayers are putting more and more pressure on legislators to cut costs. Public institutions are typically costly residential options, especially when you consider their relatively poor record in improving people's skills. Add high operating costs to the expense of rehabilitating the costly buildings and grounds (many are very old) and you have an undesirable option financially. New Jersey has announced plans to close its publicly run developmental centers. Among other reasons, they explain that it will cost about 37 million dollars by the year 2000 just to keep the buildings up to minimal federal standards for health and safety. Similar situations exist all around the country.

Some people question whether people with significant disabilities can live well in typical neighborhoods. Research shows that all people, whatever their level of functioning, thrive in the community if provided with appropriate supports. The issue is taking the form of a civil rights movement as human service technology improves. For every person who is placed in a public institution, you can find a similar person with the exact same needs living in the community with supports. The arguments for segregating people with cognitive disabilities just don't make much sense anymore. In addition, having someone live far away, surrounded by hundreds of people with disabilities and staff, is obviously going to limit social contacts. As we've been discussing, limited social contacts make an already vulnerable person even more vulnerable.

Nursing Homes

Nursing homes are typically large facilities designed to provide twenty-four-hour medical support and supervision. Optional activities are usually offered to the residents, often in a group setting.

Any training provided usually focuses on maintaining, rather than increasing, skills. So, your child won't learn to cook or budget his money in a nursing home.

Nursing homes are often one large building or a campus-style arrangement of buildings. Accommodations may include a private cottage or room or a room shared with one or two others. To qualify for admittance to a nursing home, an individual must often demonstrate a need for regular medical intervention, such as a respiration problem, a heart condition, etc. Of course, nursing homes are often filled with elderly people, which should be a consideration if you are trying to find a place for a young adult. Nursing homes can be privately or publicly funded.

Parent-Funded Alternatives

Some parents have decided to take things into their own hands and put together a "parent funded" program—that is, a program that is designed and paid for outside of the government system. These types of programs can be developed through group or individual family efforts.

One parent I know worked on expanding her son's social network and identified two college students (her son's age) who might be suitable roommates for him. She approached the two men and asked if they would be interested in providing her son with the daily support he needed in cooking and banking in exchange for free rent. The students agreed. She purchased a condominium in her son's name, outlined the support her son needed, and the three moved in together. The mother then went to the county office of mental retardation and made an agreement with the administration to provide on-going day programming in a sheltered workshop, with transportation. She also obtained an agreement for the office to help find roommates for her son if she could not and either of the two college students moved out. One or both of the students attends meetings to discuss her son's progress at the day program when requested. So far, this seems to be a happy arrangement.

A group of Jewish parents were dissatisfied with residential living arrangements they investigated because of their inability to support a Jewish lifestyle. They were also concerned because waiting lists for group homes were long and there were no guarantees that their children would be served when the parents died. They formed a non-profit organization, bought a house, and pooled their resources to staff it for a year. Six people live in the group home, each according to a Jewish lifestyle. Unfortunately, the parents have found that it is more expensive than they anticipated to staff the facility, and they are now investigating funding options. They have gone to the government for assistance but have been turned down. The last report I got was that they were going to approach a national Jewish fundraising organization for financial assistance.

Intentional Communities

Intentional communities are like communes, made up of groups of people who choose to live with people with cognitive disabilities. Sometimes people join for religious reasons. Intentional communities may be entirely self-sufficient, even to the point of raising much of their own food themselves, or may accept government or private funding. Sometimes there are paid staff, but usually any assistance needed is given freely by the capable members of the community.

Admission to intentional communities can be competitive. Examples of intentional communities which cater to people with developmental disabilities include Camphill Schools and L'Arche, which have satellites in the eastern United States. Check with your local human service agency or church for information on how to find an intentional community in your area.

There are also small communities springing up all over the country. These are well-designed housing developments with all the homes clustered around a central attraction, such as a park. Kids play together in the common area, and it becomes a focus of the community. I've never heard of a development like this designed especially for people with disabilities, but families who live in them report that there is much stronger community networking than in other neighborhoods. Each family buys their own home after being approved by a selection committee. There are no special services, just a more close-knit community. Check with local realtors for information on well-designed housing developments.

HOUSING ASSISTANCE

"I think we would like to arrange something ourselves but I don't have the money to buy a house or a condo. What kind of assistance can I get?"

There are several options for subsidizing the cost of housing, as well as for developing new housing in your community. Some of the ideas listed below will only cover part of the costs of starting a new housing project, so you may need to mix and match strategies.

Section 8 Housing

Section 8 Housing refers to assistance provided from the Department of Housing and Urban Development. HUD has two programs that offer cash subsidies to people with disabilities living on their own—rental certificates and housing vouchers.

Rental Certificates. HUD pays the difference between 30 percent of the renter's income and the fair market value of rent for the apartment. So if the renter makes $500 per month and the apartment rent is $400, the government will pay for the difference between 30 percent of $500, or $150, and $400. So the rental certificate will be for $250. Under this program, the landlord is required to charge only the Fair Market Value which is determined by HUD. Unfortunately, this is often a low rate, and many landlords are reluctant to charge such a low rental fee. This means that some of the apartments that *are* available may be run-down.

Housing Vouchers. HUD pays the difference again between 30 percent of the renter's income and the fair market value for the rental of a particular property. The difference between this and a rental certificate is that landlords can charge any rental value they want. The disadvantage of this subsidy is that the renter may have to pay a higher percentage of his income to rent to make up for the difference in rates. For example, let's say that the renter makes $500 per month and the apartment rent is $600 per month. HUD assesses the fair market value of the apartment at $400 per month and agrees to pay the difference between 30% of the renter's income ($150)

and $400, or $250. The renter must make up the difference between $600 and the $250 from the housing voucher. Therefore, the
renter must pay $350, more than half of his monthly income.

To apply for assistance from HUD, contact a HUD office in
your area. They will walk you through the application procedure and
provide you with a list of apartments available. As with most forms of
subsidized housing, there is usually a waiting list, so plan ahead.

Housing Finance Agencies (HFAS)

These organizations offer low interest loans to first-time home buy-
ers. Typically, interest rates may be 1.5 to 2 percent lower than
those of financial institutions. Sometimes, HFAs will offer interest-
free loans to people with disabilities purchasing a home for the first
time. Applicants must show that they have adequate income to support a mortgage. There is often a lot of competition for these loans,
so they may not always be available to you. To find an HFA, contact
your local government housing or community development offices
for information.

Housing Cooperatives

In a housing cooperative, a group of people purchase a house together and then share housing costs. The housing can be a condominium, an apartment building, a large house, etc. Sometimes cooperatives will accept rental certificates from HUD, or, if qualified,
the person with the disability can use housing vouchers. Some co-
ops will even exchange labor for a portion of the housing costs.

Foreclosures

Sometimes, your local HUD office will sell properties that it ac-
quires when homeowners default, or fail to pay on their loans. These
properties were insured through the Federal Housing Administration and upon foreclosure turned over to HUD. Many times, you
can purchase property very inexpensively this way. You can get a
list of available properties by contacting your local HUD office.

PASSING ON YOUR ASSETS

"I already know that I would like my son to move into a supported living arrangement with a roommate. What I'm concerned about is the money. He's good with small purchases, but I don't think he would have a clue how to manage his inheritance. I don't want to trust some social worker either. What are my options?"

When deciding how to pass money or other assets on to your child, keep in mind that you have essentially two possibilities with regards to timing: you can pass on assets while you are alive or provide for your child in your will, which goes into effect upon your death. You can also set up trust funds while you are alive, inter vivos (living) trusts, or as part of your will, referred to as a testamentary trust. One nice thing about the living trust is that you can have other people make contributions to the trust. More details on trusts follow later in this chapter.

Before deciding on any of these ideas, please review your options with a knowledgeable attorney. Laws and regulations change quickly and what's available in one state may not be available in another. Also, you need to determine how important it is not to jeopardize your child's Supplemental Security Income (SSI). Your child's assets will be calculated when the size of the SSI payment is determined. If assets are above a certain level, he will not qualify for SSI. If income from your estate will exceed monthly SSI payments, you may not be concerned about maintaining the benefit. If, however, you do want to protect your child's SSI payment, please mention this to your attorney when planning your will. In addition, some options for estates and trusts may have an impact on your taxes or carry associated administration costs which would prove cost prohibitive. Again, check with an attorney who is knowledgeable about disability and estate options.

Estates can be distributed through a variety of methods, which are detailed below:

Informal Arrangements. Informal arrangements are made without signing some kind of legal document identifying the beneficiary as the recipient of an inheritance. Usually, such an arrangement consists of the parent leaving the money to a family member or friend with the understanding that it be used for the child with the disability. Obviously, without a legal document stipulating the wishes of the parent, the child is left without any legal guarantees that the money will be used for the purpose for which it was intended.

One benefit of using this method is that it could avoid the loss of the person's government benefits, such as SSI. It may also help to avoid cost-of-care charges by state governments—charges made to the individual requiring him to pay for the cost of his own care in a state-funded facility. States typically may tap into any assets in the person's name to pay for cost of care. I have personally seen several people who have lost their entire inheritances to cost-of-care charges. When you consider that in Pennsylvania, for example, residential programs can average $60,000 a year or more, it's easy to see just how quickly an inheritance can be used up.

Special Accounts. Many financial institutions have account options which may be attractive when considering ways to leave assets to your child. For example, most banks will let you require two signatures before any money is disbursed. If someone else you designate had to sign in addition to your child, your child would be unlikely to turn his whole account over to some unscrupulous character. You could also purchase a certificate of deposit in your child's name or make him the beneficiary of a life insurance policy or annuity. Some banks offer a "Totten Trust," which allows the account balance to transfer directly to the beneficiary upon the account holder's death. A drawback of any of these ideas is that such accounts could jeopardize SSI benefits, especially if the account balance exceeds the amount allowed before SSI payments are affected.

Trusts. A trust is a legal document which allows money or property to be held for the beneficiary, and paid out in accordance with specific written instructions. Cash, personal possessions, and real estate can be put into a trust. Many parents have purchased life insurance policies on themselves, listing their child's trust as beneficiary in the event of the parent's death.

If trusts are formed when the parent is alive, the parent can serve as a trustee, or someone else can fill the role of administrator for the trust. The parent (or grantor) can also appoint a trusted person or a financial institution to serve as a trustee. It should be noted that banks and other financial institutions will charge fees to administer the trust. The trust needs to be sizeable enough to support such expenses. As with special accounts, you need to be conscious of how trusts can threaten government benefits and cost-of-care charges.

Types of Trusts

When looking into the options listed below, please keep in mind that trust laws vary from state to state. Again, you should seek the advice of an attorney when setting up a trust.

Supplemental Trust. A supplemental trust supplements the care of the person with the disability and does not supplant, or replace, government funds required to pay for this care. Therefore, the supplemental trust, if drafted properly, can protect SSI and Medicaid benefits. Allowable expenditures under this type of trust would be for items not covered by government benefits.

Discretionary Trust. In this type of trust, the trustee has full discretion over the amount of money to be distributed to the beneficiary. Sometimes, discretionary trusts will have provisions that only allow funds to go to those who supply goods or services to the person with the disability, rather than to the person himself. One possible drawback to this arrangement is that if the trustee does distribute an amount directly to the beneficiary, it will jeopardize his or her government benefits. You can check with your attorney, your local human services agency, and your Social Security office to determine an appropriate amount to leave in a discretionary trust to ensure that it will not interfere with government benefits.

Cooperative Master Trust. This is an arrangement by which several families pool their accounts. The combined account is then invested. Beneficiaries receive amounts from the trust based upon their family's percentage of the principle. For example, if the entire trust starts out at $100,000 and your family contributed $10,000, your child is entitled to 10 percent of whatever money is made through investments. This seems ideal for families who cannot afford a large trust managed by a bank. Managing the combined sum as a single account reduces administration fees. Organizations such as The Arc may assist in forming cooperative master trusts. Again, you may want to make sure that the money in the trust cannot be used for cost of care in a residential facility.

Representative Payee

Sometimes parents are concerned that their adult child with a disability may not be able to manage his government benefit check. You have the option of setting up a representative payee in such cases. Through this arrangement, the payee receives the check directly and distributes the funds for the person with the disability. Representative payees typically have to account for the way the money is spent, but it is best to make sure that the person chosen is trustworthy. You can contact your Social Security Administration office for more information.

Joint Property Ownership

If you are concerned that your child won't be able to maintain a piece of real estate or protect it from creditors, you can set up joint property ownership. This requires placing the property in the name of your child and another trusted person who could assist in the needed areas. Please be forewarned that joint property ownership could jeopardize SSI benefits.

GUARDIANSHIP

A guardian can be a particular person or a corporate entity (like a bank) who is entrusted with the care of a person (ward) who has been judged incompetent in some way. Most states have laws which allow for limited guardianship, meaning that the court can limit the control a guardian has over your son or daughter's life. For example, your son may be able to make decisions about where he wants to live and with whom, but may have a terrible time managing money.

You and your son can then work to have a particular person appointed to manage only financial issues.

Sometimes a person is judged to be completely incompetent to handle any of his affairs. The guardian, then, makes all the decisions for that person.

You can suggest a guardian in your will for a minor child, and, if uncontested, the court will most likely award guardianship to that individual. Adults who require guardianship are granted a hearing and representation to make sure that their rights are not being taken away arbitrarily. If you have guardianship of your adult child, you may want to consider naming a replacement guardian in your will. If you die and make no provisions for a guardian, anyone can petition to become your child's guardian. The court is usually careful to make sure that the person has the best interest of the "ward" at heart, and that the potential "ward" really needs someone to make decisions. Sometimes, advocacy organizations will fight guardianship requests routinely, on the basis that they unfairly remove the rights of people with developmental disabilities. If you think that your child needs a guardian, by all means, plan ahead.

Guardianship of the Person or the Property. With a guardianship of the person arrangement, the guardian is only charged with deciding personal issues, such as where to live, what services to use, whether or not to pursue medical treatment, etc. In guardianship of the property, or the estate, the conservator (guardian) only has control of assets and not personal matters. Conservators are often required by the court to protect the assets and use them for the general welfare of the beneficiary. Conservators may be required to put up a bond to show that they can be trusted to handle the funds responsibly and they may need to invest assets.

Limited Guardianship. This type of guardianship allows the guardian's control to be limited according to the individual's needs, thereby allowing the person with the disability to maintain as much control as possible over his own life. You may want to limit the person's ability to make financial decisions, for example. As with trusts, guardianship laws vary from state to state and limited guardianship may not be an option for you. Check with an attorney.

Full Guardianship. This is the strictest guardianship arrangement, giving the guardian control over all aspects of the ward's life. This might be appropriate for someone who is completely incapacitated (e.g., in a coma), but is not recommended for a person with mental retardation who can give input into decisions about programming and lifestyle. Unfortunately, there are still a few states in the country which offer only full guardianship, with no opportunities for limited arrangements. A person who lives under full guardianship has very few legal rights and will have to obtain the guardian's consent on all major decisions. Advocates often work with people with cognitive disabilities to fight a petition for full guardianship by providing expert witnesses who testify that people with such disabilities can and do make responsible decisions. In most states, a full guardianship arrangement can be dissolved, as can other guardianship arrangements, through a court proceeding.

Temporary Guardianship. Sometimes the court will issue temporary guardianship or a "protective order" when someone is temporarily incapacitated, usually due to illness. This gives another person or a social service agency the ability to handle a specific legal problem, such as making medical decisions. This arrangement is not designed for long-term guardianship problems, as guardianship is removed after the specific legal problem is addressed.

Where to Find Guardians

"HELP! I've looked everywhere for a guardian and no one seems to measure up. What can I do?"

The first thing I would suggest is going back over Chapters Three, Four, and Five and trying those suggestions. It's downright risky for a person with a disability to be so isolated. It will be better for your child if he has several strong advocates who can look out for him after you die.

You may also be a little harsh in your assessment of who would make a good guardian. The Arc, a national organization on mental retardation, offers "A Family Handbook on Future Planning" which has a lot of useful information for parents and helped me greatly in coming up with the information for this chapter. The handbook includes a checklist of qualities which make for a good guardian:

- Lives relatively close to the ward
- Has enough time to assist the person and carry out responsibilities
- Is willing to learn about new programs for people with mental retardation
- Is willing to adapt to changing circumstances
- If it is a guardianship of the estate, has good property management abilities.

Public Guardianship. Some local or state government agencies provide guardianship services directly or may contract with a non-profit organization. Such options are usually recommended only as a last resort. This is because the staff charged with the guardianship or trusteeship duties often have large caseloads, a lot of paperwork, and duties which may compete with attending to your son or daughter. It's almost always better to find your own guardian, someone who knows your child and can devote the amount of time necessary to his situation.

Corporate Guardianship. Basically, corporate guardianship programs are companies that sell guardianship services, contracting with interested families for guardianship services. Payment can be arranged several different ways, with many companies encouraging the use of life insurance to establish the principle for the account upon your death. The corporation is named as the guardian for the individual, with staff carrying out specific duties relating to each case. Corporate guardianships is not available in all parts of the country.

Guardians for Minors

"My son is four years old. Aren't the guardianship laws different for a child?"

Good point. All parents of minors should make provisions in their wills for a guardian. If you die, guardianship is usually transferred to the surviving parent. If both parents die, the court will appoint a guardian to look after the child until he reaches the "age of maturity."

Guardians for children are usually different from guardians for adults because they are usually expected to act like a parent for the child.

Oftentimes, the court will follow a list of people recommended by the parents in their will. If the parents failed to recommend somebody, the court may appoint a social services agency or someone who is willing and capable of accepting the child. Guardians are sometimes required to meet court-specified qualifications, which vary from state to state and case to case. Contact a knowledgeable attorney or your local children and youth agency to find out more.

Make certain that as your child grows and his situation changes, you update your will. For example, when your child turns 21, you may no longer want or need a guardian. You may find that your child has obtained the skills and the maturity he needs to make these decisions on his own. If so, consider yourself fortunate and delete the guardianship provision of your will.

CHAPTER **11**

WHEN SHOULD I MAKE SOME OF THESE CHANGES?

"My twenty-year-old daughter, Amanda, has so many friends I worry that she spreads herself too thin! She's been pestering me to move in with a friend of hers who seems willing. I didn't expect things to move this fast. Should we go ahead or should I keep her with me until I become unable to care for her?"

O nce you have begun to put the pieces of your child's support network in place and have settled on a place for her to live, what should your next move be? I strongly advocate making the changes as soon as you and your child feel ready and have the resources. There are several good reasons to do this while the parents are healthy and able to be supportive.

Reason 1. What if it doesn't work out? Parents can act as the ultimate safety net for a child going out into the world for the first time. A lot of us support children who don't have disabilities in this way. So many children have trouble adjusting to an independent lifestyle that they've even developed a new term, "boomerangers," to describe the phenomenon.

There are many potential "bugs" in your child's new life that may need to be worked out. For example, your child may not be happy with her new roommates or may find support staff too pushy and restrictive. She may not like living in the city as much as she thought she would or her roommate may have to move out. All kinds of things can happen.

It's possible that you may think you have found the perfect person to look out for your child, but then find out that you're mistaken. For example, Joan was delighted when she asked Leonard to be her son's advocate and he agreed immediately to the role. Then, shortly after the commitment, Joan's son, Paul, seemed to become dissatisfied with his outings with Leonard. Paul said that Leonard had started to boss him around and wasn't as much fun as he used to be. Joan encouraged Paul to talk to Leonard about his complaints. Paul did so, but the situation didn't improve. Joan then talked to Leonard herself. Leonard justified his behavior by saying that he felt he should play a more responsible role in Paul's life now. Joan isn't sure at this point what she should do; should she encourage Leonard's new place in Paul's life or should she start looking around for someone else?

In my opinion, even if Leonard was the perfect advocate for Lawrence and the two got along famously, Joan should still look around for other candidates. What if something happened to Leonard? What would happen to Lawrence then? Also, if the relationship has ceased to be pleasurable for Lawrence, chances are that it is also less pleasurable for Leonard. This relationship may dissolve before long.

The point is, if you're available, you can help ease your child through some of the crises that are bound to come up and ease the transition into her new lifestyle. You can also start all over with some different ideas, if necessary.

Reason 2. Parents can provide emotional support. Parental support can make the difference between a successful and an unsuccessful lifestyle change. Sometimes all your child needs is the emotional security of knowing that Mom and Dad are available if something goes wrong. How many of us have sent a child off to college and gotten seven phone calls the first week, five the second, and none when she got a boyfriend? It can be hard to be away from Mom and Dad at first, but many children will learn to rely on others for that day-to-day emotional support.

Reason 3. Parents can provide other types of support. My mom used to slip me a couple of bucks every now and then when my cash was running low. If my sister didn't have any food in the house, she knew she could show up at Mom's around dinner time and still get fed. My mom buys all kinds of things for the grandchildren—toys, extra Easter candy, clothes, stuff they wouldn't get otherwise. I can't tell you how many of my friends do their kids' laundry. Sometimes these little things can really help someone get over a rough spot. If your child moves out and you can help her survive by slipping her a couple of bucks and doing her laundry, consider yourself ahead of the game.

Reason 4. Parents can help work out the nuts and bolts of a new lifestyle. A friend of mine with a disability purchased his own home, found a housemate, and had a nice group of people to socialize with, but couldn't figure out transportation to his supported employment position. Unfortunately, the county office that was supposed to facilitate his involvement in the work program was unwilling to help work out a solution. The guy's parents got involved and turned the system upside down. They contacted legislators, went to city council meetings, and were such effective advocates that the county office acquiesced and agreed to provide transportation for as long as it was needed.

Some other details that parents have worked out ahead of time include finding a job or day program for their child, setting up housekeeping assistance, and arranging for medical care or bill paying.

Reason 5. Parents can ensure that their child is happy and secure. Karen placed her daughter Mary Jane in a family living program. Mary Jane has severe mental retardation and physical disabilities. She doesn't speak and only those who know her really well can tell if she's comfortable and happy. Karen visited her daughter regularly and soon noticed that whenever she popped in unannounced, Mary Jane would be lying on her back in bed with dirty hair and dirty clothes. She also noticed that Mary Jane was becoming less and less attentive. Karen raised her concerns with the family living provider, who responded defensively. Things got a little better for a while but soon went back to the same old thing. Karen then took her concerns to the manager of the program and requested a new provider. Fortunately, the manager agreed to a change. Mary Jane moved in with the new family and things seem much better.

This story illustrates the role you can play in making sure that a new living arrangement meets your child's needs. Parents' viewpoints are often so valued in the social service system that some states actively encourage parents to monitor community living arrangements on a regular basis. It's felt that parents can monitor their child's quality of life much better than a government agency can. Government agencies are primarily concerned with making sure that a particular living situation meets government regulations.

Visit your child's home and ask yourself the following:

- Does it seem like a place you'd like to live in? If no, why not?
- Is your child happy? Healthy? Does she resist returning to her new home?
- Is the place clean? Homey? Does it smell good?
- Does she have her own things on the walls, choose her meals, and watch what she likes on television? Or does someone else make all the decisions?
- Does she go out often and have contact with nondisabled people?
- Does she look nice? Does she still have all her clothes and are they neatly stored? Is she well groomed?
- Does she seem depressed, moody, or withdrawn? Why?
- Does she still see her friends and participate in her favorite activities? Why or why not?

    ✐ In general, does she seem to be thriving and
       growing? Or going backwards?

If your quick check reveals any problems, and she lives in a residential program, work with the staff to resolve the issue. If she is on her own, or has a roommate, you'll need to take the lead in helping her solve the problem. Involve your child's support person or persons, if possible.

Reason 6. Parents can lend needed credibility to friends who will be advocating for their child. The social service system can be a closed system to people outside of the family unit. Providers of services may justifiably be concerned about sharing sensitive information with people who are not related to the person with the disability. Unfortunately, this concern can keep the person isolated and prevent those who can help from getting the information, such as medical information or behavior management techniques, they need to resolve a particular problem.

When you have identified someone who is willing and able to advocate for your child after you die, you will want to begin introducing him or her to the system now. This will help in several ways: 1) social workers will become used to seeing your child's support person and having her involved in program planning sessions; 2) providers will recognize the person as having some clout and status; and 3) the friend will begin to learn how to deal with the system effectively. If you continually have problems getting the system to recognize the friend, try appealing decisions to keep the friend at a distance. If you've gone all the way up and down the decision-making ladder with no success, you may, as a last resort, want to consider having the person appointed as a guardian.

Reason 7. It will be easier on your child if she can adjust to a new lifestyle while you are still alive. If the move is held off until your death, your child will have to cope with too much all at once. People with disabilities grieve. Sometimes people feel that because someone has mental retardation or autism, they aren't going to feel an intense loss when someone close to them dies. This is just not true. People with cognitive disabilities may have some difficulty with the abstract coping mechanisms that many of us use to ease our suffering, but they grieve nonetheless.

Researchers Jim Turner and Joseph Graffam have documented one similarity between the way people with and without mental retardation grieve. In an article in the *American Journal of Mental Retardation*, they reported that there are no real differences in the dreams that people with mental retardation have about deceased loved ones and those that the rest of us have.

Grieving is often thought of as a process. Depending upon the circumstances surrounding the death, people will be at different stages of the grieving process. Elisabeth Kubler-Ross, probably the most famous authority on death and dying today, identified five stages of the emotional process surrounding death:

Denial & Isolation. The first emotional stage usually involves a reaction of disbelief. The person who is dying or his or her family members may assume that a fatal condition is just a temporary problem or that dying is something that only happens to other people.

Anger. After denial comes a realization that death is indeed imminent. There is often a lot of anger about the prognosis. People will ask, "Why me?" They will compare themselves to someone who is not facing death and ask why that person should be spared.

Bargaining. Family members going through this stage try to negotiate for the dying person's life. "Maybe if I'm very good, my mother won't die," or "Maybe if she makes it until Thanksgiving, they'll change the prognosis."

Depression. At this point, the dying person or her family members realize that nothing they do will be able to prevent the person from dying. A sense of great loss sets in.

Acceptance. Finally, there is an acceptance of the impending death which is almost completely void of feelings. The emotional pain surrounding the event is gone and the dying person or the family member feels a sense of peace.

Kubler-Ross says that family members may also feel guilt and wish to make up for past missed experiences with the dying person. For example, a daughter may regret never taking her father to lunch or telling him how much she loves him. If the death was particularly painful or drawn out, family members may feel a sense of euphoria that it's finally over. Again, they will probably feel guilty about their euphoric reaction. Kubler-Ross recommends letting family members talk about their feelings and accepting them, regardless of what they are.

Of course, depending on the skills available to your child with a cognitive disability, these stages and feelings may be expressed in different ways. Some people become withdrawn, others revert to old habits such as over-eating or smoking, some become aggressive, and still others do all of these at different points in the process.

The duration of the grief process also varies. Some people bounce back in about three months after losing a parent; others take years to work through all of their feelings.

Families can help the person with the disability see death as a natural part of the life cycle and provide models for coping effectively with grief. One of the best ways to do this is to allow the person in on family funerals and rituals as they occur throughout life. Many parents exclude their children with disabilities from such events—but think about what this can lead to. You just lost your mother, you've never been to a funeral before, and all these people are coming up to you and saying things about your mother. Who wouldn't be confused and overwhelmed in such a situation?

There is so much stress surrounding the death of a parent that whatever you can do to prepare your child is probably useful. Some families take comfort in certain religious rituals that occur when someone dies. It's possible that your child will also be able to take some comfort in such rituals, but she needs to be exposed to them first. Still others may just need to know that it's okay to cry in public and be sad when your parents die.

You may also want to give your child's friends some ideas on how to support your child through the grieving process, as in the example below.

> Shortly after Gary moved in with John, his mother died. Gary started to do some strange things, such as washing his hands repeatedly, closing doors, and checking and rechecking to make sure the doors were closed. Fortunately, Gary's mother had told John that Gary did these things when he was under a lot of stress. John just waited things out and tried to make sure that Gary experienced few changes in his routine for several months. Gary eventually decreased his compulsive behavior.

Fortunately, John knew enough about Gary to see him through a difficult period in his life. It's easy to over-react when you see a person you care about doing strange things. John could have easily assumed that Gary needed more intensive support than John could provide. As it turned out, all Gary needed was an opportunity to work through his feelings, and some added stability to his lifestyle.

IT'S NEVER TOO EARLY

"My son, Samuel, is only four years old. I don't think that he's going to have to deal with my death for some time yet. I'm not going to have him move out on his own, obviously. Besides making sure I have a guardian appointed to look out for him, is there anything I should be doing to help prepare for the future or should I just not worry about it until he's older?"

It's never too early to begin working on your child's social contacts. Many people feel that the earlier you start mixing kids with and without disabilities, the easier it will be to overcome negative attitudes and stereotypes later in life. One parent told me that not only was it important for her daughter with Down syndrome to have nondisabled kids for friends, it was important for the nondisabled kids to know her daughter as well. She pointed out that these people will be legislators and school board members and voters when they grow up. An early understanding of what people with disabilities want and need will undoubtedly make advocacy a lot easier in the future.

Other helpful things that parents can do right away include:

- Get involved with an advocacy group to become more knowledgeable on issues facing your child. See Chapter 12 for more information.
- Become more involved in your community yourself. Anything you do to increase your own contacts could ultimately benefit your child.
- Involve your child in all aspects of community life, not just school. Try tee ball, the local community center, etc.

- Work with provider agencies to get new residential programs started in your community. Sometimes, providers are slow to develop new types of service because they think there is no demand for them. Show them that you are interested and willing to help.
- If you think your child will need a residential program, make sure to get her on a waiting list for such services early. You can contact your local government human services agency for more information.
- Plan your estate and write a will because you never know when you might die.
- Make sure that the guardian you name in your will knows your hopes and dreams for your child's future.

CHAPTER 12

WHAT IF I CAN'T GET THE SUPPORT I NEED?

"My daughter lives in a public institution, which is the only service anywhere around here. I want to set her up in her own home and have some support staff help her out several times a week. The local social service agency says they don't have any money for that. What can I do to get them to help us out?"

❖

"I took my daughter with me to the health club. I figured she and I could both get in shape while we worked on making new friends. The health club manager came over and said he wasn't sure if she could work out because of his insurance liability. I'm really angry! What should I do?"

❖

"My son lives at home. I would like him to move into a house with two other guys and see how he likes it. Social services tells me that they don't have any funding for group homes and that they will place him on a waiting list. I know

*that waiting list has about 200 people on it. Is there
something I can do to speed things up?"*

❖

*"My daughter lives in an eight-person group home. She
wants to get a job, I think she can do it, and the staff at the
day program thinks she would be good. Her group home
manager, however, says that she can't make any money or
he'll have to throw her out of the group home. What kind of
crazy system is this?"*

The inflexibility of large bureaucracies, prejudice against people
who are different, competition for money, government regulations—
all of these things and countless others can throw a monkey wrench
into the best-laid plans. Consequently, you need to be prepared to
work on behalf of your child—to become his advocate. Experienced parent advocates will encourage you to believe in your child
and to believe in your own ability to know what's best for your
child. And it's true that no one knows your child better than you
do. When you feel intimidated by someone's credentials, remember that no one has the years of experience that you have in working with your son or daughter.

You need to take care of yourself when you are fighting for
something for your child. Recruit allies, seek out information,
take advantage of a sympathetic ear. Pat yourself on the back
when you make a little bit of progress. When you have set-
backs, pat yourself on the back for hanging in there. Anyone
with any experience in advocacy will tell you that change takes
time. And guts.

Expect to be in this fight for the long haul. Even if you get
everything you want for your child, you need to remain up-to-date
on what's happening to prevent an erosion of services. There are
many national trends that could chip away at funding for the supports that your child needs. For example, there's a lot of emphasis
now on cost containment. This means that legislators are inclined
to place caps on funding for services. Caps on funding mean that
there will be waiting lists for those services. Parents need to let
legislators know how badly services are needed for their children.

If they don't hear from parents, legislators will listen to groups that want these programs cut.

BECOMING AN ADVOCATE

Problems come in all shapes and sizes. They can be as large as a national trend or as small as a bigoted health club manager. Expect problems to arise as you begin to make changes, and hone your advocacy skills.

How you approach a particular problem depends on the type of problem, the resources at your disposal, and your particular advocacy style.

The Parent Education Network and the Pennsylvania Coalition for Citizens with Disabilities put together a training program for parent advocates of school-age children with disabilities. Much of the information is relevant to assisting your child in making lifestyle changes. Their guide, *In Praise of Parents*, lists three types of advocacy used by parents:

Individual Advocacy. Individual advocacy includes activities designed to assist your own child. Goals for this type of advocacy may include getting your child a communication device or finding a suitable residential program. Activities might include meeting with professionals who are involved with your child's care, participating in planning sessions, and educating your family, friends, and community about your child's disability. Skills needed to be successful in this type of advocacy include communication skills, knowledge of disability laws and regulations, and knowledge about disability.

Class Advocacy. Class advocacy refers to advocacy aimed at benefiting a larger group directly and your child indirectly. Goals may include improving conditions at a residential facility or changing a policy so that people with disabilities can take part in activities at a local community center. Activities might include sitting on advisory boards, making presentations to advisory boards, and participating in other relevant organizations that make policy recommendations. Skills needed for this type of advocacy include problem-solving skills to identify issues or sources of resistance, communication skills, and specific knowledge about disabilities.

Systems Advocacy. This term refers to activities that are aimed at changing service systems on a local, state, or national level. Some goals of systems advocacy might be changing regulations to allow for a new type of residential program or increasing the amount people can have in their bank accounts before their government benefits are reduced. Activities include educating legislators on issues, lobbying, commenting on legislation, participating in class action suits, writing letters to the editor, conducting media campaigns, etc. Useful skills for systems advocates include being able to problem-solve to identify the real issue and where to put pressure, and understanding the legal system, the political system, and the media.

BECOMING AN EFFECTIVE ADVOCATE

The Parent Education Network also offers a checklist of ideas that can spur your creativity in looking for approaches to solve your problems. A modified version of the list is below:

1. Become knowledgeable about your child's rights. You can get information about advocating and legal rights from other parents, the bar association, the American Civil Liberties Union, your legislator, or any of several national disability advocacy groups. (See Appendix C.) If you are having problems with a social service, you can contact them directly and ask for their grievance or complaint procedures. If you are having problems with your child's school, the Individuals with Disabilities Education Act provides a formal procedure for negotiating problems called "due process." You can find additional information on your "due process" rights from your state department of education or an attorney skilled in special education law. If a business or public agency is discriminating against your child, you may have recourse under the Americans with Disabilities Act (ADA).

The importance of knowing your rights cannot be emphasized too much. At the beginning of this chapter, we looked at an example of a rights violation at a health club. Facilities that offer services to the public, such as the health club, must make accommodations for people with disabilities, despite what their insurance plans say. This type of access is guaranteed under the Americans with Disabilities Act. Most areas have a Human Relations Commission which can help point you in the right direction if you are experiencing problems and don't know where to start resolving them. Simply check your phone book, call up, and explain the situation.

2. Keep records in one place. One parent I know gets really irritated because every time she applies to a service they ask for the same huge amount of information. She keeps it all, evaluations, test results, program plans, log books in a four-drawer filing cabinet. It helps her to keep everything in one place so she can refer back to things that were recommended and not followed up on, what's been tried in the past, etc. I recommend that you, too, devise a method of keeping your child's educational, medical, and other records organized so that you can quickly put your hands on the information you need.

3. Get it in writing. If they promise you something, get it in writing to ensure that they deliver. If they deny you something, get it in writing, so that you can show it to others if necessary. Also, whenever you are dissatisfied, put your dissatisfaction in writing. Nothing gets attention like a letter. Keep a copy for yourself in your child's file.

4. Keep a telephone log. Whenever you make a call about your child to an agency, note the date, time, what you discussed, and with whom. This will help you follow up and give additional credibility if you have to write a letter.

5. Go to meetings prepared. Reviewing meeting materials beforehand will help you formulate questions to ask, as well as any objections you may want to make. If you're going to a program planning meeting, bring a list of things you would like to see addressed in the upcoming year. If you don't think people will be responsive to your suggestions, be prepared with your reasons for making the requests. If you are fighting for a new service, you may want to bring along experts who can testify on why your child needs such a program. Pass around your own sign-in sheet so that you have a record of who attended the meeting.

6. Take a friend. A parent I know says, "Never go alone." She feels that parents need the emotional support of another person when they walk into the room and are often faced with several professionals. Even if that other person does nothing in the meeting, it can be a comfort just knowing that someone else is on your side. If you brief your friend ahead of time, he or she can also help make sure you cover everything you intended to at the meeting.

7. Be a good communicator. Be assertive and make sure you communicate clearly what you want. Get a clear understanding of what's being agreed upon and what the next step is.

8. Know when enough is enough! Sometimes you just can't get an acceptable resolution to a problem. Sometimes you are going to get angry. That's fine and perfectly normal. Be honest about your feelings. If necessary, call a halt to the meeting and reschedule it for another time. On your own or with friends, work out ways of getting more support for your position. Recognize, too, that sometimes you will have to take further steps to resolve a problem to your satisfaction.

Key Points about Assertive Communication

As discussed above, one cornerstone of effective advocacy is clear, assertive communication. The Parent Education Network offers these suggestions for effective communication. Assertive Communication is:

- **Self-expressive**—Don't hesitate to tell people what you and your child want. It's the only way they're going to be able to respond to your needs.
- **Respectful of the rights of others**—Make sure that others get to speak their mind as well.
- **Honest**—People will respect you more easily if you make sure your facts are accurate and consistent.
- **Direct and firm**—Don't allow yourself to be distracted by excuses for inaction. Be clear about what you need and talk to people who can make the appropriate decisions.
- **Verbal**—using words to effectively convey the content of the message (feelings, rights, facts,

opinions, requests, limits)—If you're angry, say so. Don't assume that people will know what you're thinking and feeling just by looking at you.

- **Nonverbal**—delivered in a style that helps to get the message across (eye contact, voice, posture, facial expression, gestures, distance, timing, listening)—Wave your arms, make faces, raise your eyebrows in addition to telling people how you feel. A little drama can go a long way.

- **Appropriate for the person or situation; not universal**—Don't expect a direct care staff person to be able to solve your financial problems. Make sure that you target the correct person to solve a particular problem. Go to a supervisor for staffing changes, an accountant for finances, etc.

- **Learned, not inborn**—Some parents look at experienced parent advocates and say, "I could never do that. I'm just not natured that way." But if you talk to the experienced advocates, you find that they feel that they acquired their assertiveness and strength of character through their efforts on behalf of their children. Advocates are made, they say, not born.

Finding Support

Another cornerstone to effective advocacy is finding allies—people who will support you in your advocacy efforts. Here are some places to find other advocates.

FAMILY/FRIENDS

Take your sister to a meeting and your mom to meet with a legislator. Family members are often happy to be involved and to help demonstrate to others that a number of people care about your child. Your friends can also help. A group of parents I know were all going through the education system's due process procedures at the same time. They decided to support each other by attending each other's due process hearings. They sometimes acted outrageously at these hearings and did things like make faces of disbelief or outrage when the school district testified and applauded every time the parents spoke. I don't know if they influenced the hearing officer, but they were very successful. More importantly, several of those parents told me that they would not have had the intestinal fortitude to face the considerable resources of the school district on their own. I've heard that there are similar little groups like this all over the place. For instance, *US News and World Report* did an article on a group in California which called themselves "Mothers From Hell."

LEGISLATORS/ELECTED OFFICIALS

Public servants are often well-meaning people who have the resources to cut through bureaucracy. Meet with your elected officials, introduce your child, and explain the problem you're having. I've seen a lot of parents use the influence of an elected official to learn about their options, put them in touch with the right person, or cut through a waiting list. Give it a shot!

Also, take the time to visit these folks when you have a service that is functioning nicely for you. Saying thanks goes a long way with legislators. They need to hear that tax dollars are being effectively spent so that they can make informed budget decisions in the future. If your son is working through supported employment, for example, take the time to tell a legislator of his success. You never know when a particular program is going to be considered for funding cuts.

Parents have been able to accomplish some amazing things when they've entered into a partnership with legislators. In California, parents were able to achieve entitlement to rehabilitative services for people with developmental disabilities. The Lanterman Act is the only such legislation of its kind in the United States, fought for and won by parent advocates. Unfortunately, it's constantly under attack because entitlement can be expensive. Parent advocates in California are constantly working to make sure that the Lanterman Act isn't eroded.

In New Jersey, parent advocates fought for funding to address that state's waiting lists for services. Several millions of dollars were obtained through a large bond issue. Similar battles for funding are occurring throughout the country.

Key legislators responsible for these victories will all tell you the same thing; they have somehow been personally touched by a person with a disability. Either they have someone with a disability in their families, or they have a constituent who took the time to educate them. Legislators can be important allies for parent advocates. Take the time to visit yours today.

SELF ADVOCACY GROUPS

These are groups that are comprised primarily of people with disabilities, with a few nondisabled people acting in supportive roles. The groups are growing in number and are available in many parts of the country. The membership of each develops its own agenda, usually focusing on situations experienced by its members. Many members say that, through the group, they learned how to better communicate their feelings about social services, enabling them to make changes in their own lives.

There are some risks involved in self advocacy. For whatever reasons, the social service system likes participants who are compliant and easy to deal with. People—with or without disabilities—aren't terribly popular when they complain about something. The problem is magnified when the person has a cognitive disability and is living in a residential program, reliant on the program for almost all his needs. Sometimes the system will punish the person for speaking up and try to force him back into compliancy.

Self advocacy groups also occasionally fall prey to manipulative support people. These support people can have good or questionable motivations for their behavior. The end result, however, is that the group begins to be a vehicle for expressing the needs or perspectives of the support person and ceases to be a reflection of the membership. It's pretty easy to spot when this type of thing is happening. You start to see the group push agendas using social service jargon or philosophize about abstract human service concepts. For example, I once gave a ride to a young man with mental retardation who was the president of a local self advocacy group. He was on his way to a local television station to be interviewed. On the way over, he was going through his list of things to discuss and mentioned "House Bill 711." I asked him to describe the bill. He said he didn't know what it was, but his advisor said the group was against it and he should mention it. Most people with cognitive disabilities that I know tend to be very concrete, and, like the rest of us, are concerned with getting a good job, being able to go out when they want to, and knowing how to deal with the difficult people in their life.

CITIZEN ADVOCACY

In citizen advocacy, a non-profit organization matches a nondisabled person with a person with a disability, following a structured set of guidelines. Typically, one or two paid staff members identify, screen, and match people with disabilities to popular, well-connected, and respected members of the community. The nondisabled person is usually referred to as the "mentor" and the person with the disability is often described as the "protégé." The mentor is usually recruited to help the protégé solve a specific problem such as finding a job, straightening out finances, changing living arrangements, etc. The guidelines for citizen advocacy programs were developed by John O'Brien from Georgia and include requirements that matches must be made outside of the social service system, must occur within a specific town or neighborhood, and other stipulations. One drawback of Citizen Advocacy programs is the low number of people matched each year, usually ten to twenty per office.

FRIEND ADVOCACY

This is a less structured version of citizen advocacy, but it still revolves around matching people up, one on one. A major flaw in these types of advocacy is the same problem you will face if you help your child develop only one friendship. What happens if something happens to that one person? We live in a transient society; people move and relationships change all the time. Still and all, citizen and friend advocacy programs can be useful in helping you resolve a particular problem you may be facing. The people who run these programs often have contacts in the community you may not have and are knowledgeable about disability rights.

PARENT GROUPS

There are several national advocacy organizations, including The Arc and United Cerebral Palsy, which may have local chapters in your community. If not, you can always contact their national offices (see Appendix C) for suggestions about resolving a problem. Oftentimes these groups have a professional advocate on their staff who can assist you with specific problems. If no staff member is available, you can ask them to hook you up with other parents in the area who may have dealt with the same situation. At a minimum, a parent organization can help you find other groups in the area who may be willing to help address your problem.

There are, of course, drawbacks to parent groups. Probably the biggest problem is that some groups may exist more to meet the agendas of parents than of people with disabilities. Keep this in mind, should you decide to sign up. Many have membership fees which entitle you to newsletters, invitations to conferences, etc.

COMPUTER NETWORKS

With the popularity of computer bulletin board services, online disability support groups are now pretty common. America Online has a disability group, with special sections for parents, people interested in inclusion, Arc members, etc. One of the most exciting groups is Parent Panthers, a group of courageous parents who really support each other as they make changes in their children's lives. Other services, including CompuServe, have similar support groups.

In addition to the major online services, you can also take advantage of several "usenet groups" related to disabilities on the Internet. The Internet Yellow Pages lists twenty-one different groups on all kinds of disability issues, from the Americans with Disabilities Act to Fathers of Children with Disabilities to resources for people who are mentally retarded and deaf. Some of these resources are listings of smaller services. For example, "Handicap BBS Lists" is a list of more than eight hundred computer bulletin board services that you can dial directly.

If you're extremely busy and just can't find the time to get out to a parent meeting, you may want to get a computer with a modem and stay current through such online services. Some of the groups I monitor have helped parents with advice on how to handle negative teachers, where to find adaptive equipment, and what's happening with federal legislation.

A major advantage of online services is that you can post a question and people are more than willing to try to help you out. You don't have to make five phone calls to find out where to get a good communication device, for example. You can simply post a message and come back a couple of days later to find that someone has thoughtfully provided the answer.

A lot of emotional support is given out online as well. While this is helpful (we can use all the support we can get), I don't think it quite takes the place of meeting other parents face to face. Still, it's a source of information not to be neglected by the well-informed parent advocate.

Getting online is relatively easy nowadays; many new computers are sold with software that makes hooking up pretty easy.

PROTECTION AND ADVOCACY OFFICES

Each state has a Protection and Advocacy office, required by federal legislation. The job of the P & A is to advocate for people with disabilities, including people who are mentally ill. Many offices address system-wide problems as well as individual complaints of abuse. Protection and Advocacy offices have the power to review records and monitor facilities. Some of them fund public interest law firms in addition to their own staff. P & A advocates are usually knowledgeable about the problems and successes of the social service system in a particular state. Many provide information on how you can address a particular problem.

PARENTING IS NOT FOR COWARDS

All this talk about what can go wrong and how to marshal your forces could make you want to forget the whole thing. It's tempting to let things continue as they always have been, to keep your child comfortably isolated, and to try not to think too much about the future. Maybe you'll outlive him.

And maybe not.

You can't be a parent today and not have heard some awful story about a person with a disability left alone in the world. The person who was taken away from his home and thrown in an institution somewhere out in no man's land. The person living on the street. The person who falls prey to con artists or rapists or muggers. The person who's just so unhappy that whenever someone comes to see him, he begs, "please get me out of here." The person in a residential facility who is dressed shabbily and has a dead, vacant expression on his face.

As we've seen, you can't really rely on residential programs and staff to make sure your child is happy and secure. What you may be able to rely on is the involvement of other people. If staff and service providers see that your child is loved and watched over, they will be much more likely to provide good service. Staff are busy people. Who are they likely to spend time on? Someone who has a visitor coming today or the person no one ever sees? This isn't an indictment of staff; it's just plain common sense. If no one ever asks about Joe, who is likely to get a little shortchanged when staff is busy? If Martha's advocate comes to visit on a regular basis, and regularly addresses problems when they arise, isn't it likely that staff is going to make sure that Martha is treated pretty well? Of course, your child could be in a residential program where everyone is treated equally, but it just makes sense to try to make sure that your child is as well networked as possible.

What I've tried to do with this book is to bring the latest thinking about supporting people with disabilities directly to parents. I have seen some professionals who reject some of this thinking and therefore don't pass it on to parents. The rejection stems from a variety of reasons. Administrators may be concerned about how this new thinking will affect their own out-dated services, or just have so many other pressures on them that they can't take the time to build networks around people. Administrators, like direct care staff, have a lot of things that compete for their time. It would be nice if your child's happiness was their number one priority, but that's not always true.

Following the advice in this book may make you a little uncomfortable as well. It may be hard to shake up some of the professionals and family members in your child's life. Many parents tell me that they were never very assertive until they had a child with a disability. Now these formerly meek people are the lions of the disability movement, giving testimony before legislators and encouraging other parents to fight the good fight. These are the people who are responsible for many of the advances in the disability movement we enjoy today—The Individuals with Disabilities Education Act, the Americans with Disabilities Act, the Rehabilitation Act. The disability movement has evolved tremendously over the last twenty-five years, largely due to the courage of parents just like you.

It's time now to see that people with disabilities enjoy full participation in our communities. It's not enough to have the legal right to join some club or to go to public school; people with disabilities want to truly *belong*. There isn't any court that can make another child invite your child to a birthday party or have him over for a barbecue. This is the next arena. We have to help people abandon their odd notions about people with disabilities and begin to see them the way we do—as warm, giving individuals. The only way that will happen is if people come together, one by one, face to face.

That's what this book is all about. Getting people together, face to face. I hope that you will have the courage to continue building people into your child's life. The stakes are just too high not to. Good luck!

APPENDIX A

PUBLICATIONS ABOUT WILLS, ESTATES, AND TRUSTS

Please be aware that laws governing inheritance and guardianship vary from state to state. Check with an attorney in your own state when making your arrangements. Also, keep in mind that your guardian will make all the difference in your child's life. Choose that person carefully.

Alternatives to Public Guardianship: Models of Protective Services. Columbus, OH: Advocacy and Protective Services, 1986. Includes a survey of 50 states on guardianship law. Available from Advocacy and Protective Services, Inc., 986 W. Goodale Blvd., Columbus, OH 43212, (614) 469-9615, 1-800-282-9363.

Directory of Lawyer Referral Services. Chicago, American Bar Association (750 N. Lakeshore Dr., Chicago, IL, 60611), 1988. ($3.50).

Estate and Financial Planning for the Aging or Incapacitated Client. D.P. Callahan & P.J. Strauss. New York: Practicing Law Institute, 1988. (D4-5199 - $45.00).

Estate Planning. J. A. Manning. New York: Practicing Law Institute, 1988. (D1 - 0156 - $85.00).

A Family Handbook on Future Planning. Richard Berkobien. Arlington, TX: The Arc, Department of Research and Program Services, 1991. Each copy is $15.00.

Financial Planning for the Handicapped. D.P. Holdren. Springfield, IL: Charles C. Thomas Publishing Co., 1985. ($32.50).

Guardianship for Citizens with Developmental Disabilities: A Training Package for Guardians. Lansing, MI: Michigan Protection and Advocacy Service, 1984. Available from Michigan Protection and Advocacy, 313 S. Washington Square, Suite 050, Lansing MI 48933, (517) 487-1755, 1-800-292-5923.

How to Provide for Their Future: Suggestions for Parents Concerned with Providing Lifetime Support for a Child with a Developmental Disability. Prepared by The Arc of the United States Insurance Committee, Arlington, TX, 1989. Each copy is $10.00. Write for your copies at:

> The Arc of the United States
> 500 East Border St., Suite 300
> Arlington, Texas 76010
> (817) 261-6003

Life Services Planning - Training Volunteers and Practitioners. Chicago: American Bar Association, 1987.

A New Look at Guardianship and Protective Services that Support Personalized Living. T. Apolloni & T.P. Cooke. Baltimore: Paul H. Brookes Publishing Co., 1984. ($24.95).

"Persons with Severe Mental Retardation and the Limits of Guardian Decision-Making." Robert M. Veatch. In: **Ethics of Dealing with Persons with Severe Handicap,** P.R. Dokecki & R.M. Zaner, Editors. Baltimore: Paul H. Brookes Publishing Co., 1986.

Setting Up and Executing Trusts. A.D. Sederbaum. New York: Practicing Law Institute, 1988. (Q1 - 3005 - $50.00).

RESOURCES FOR PLANNING FOR THE FUTURE

Books and Publications on Person-Centered Planning

Alternatives: A Family Guide to Legal and Financial Planning for the Disabled. L.M. Russell. Evanston: First Publications, Inc. (P.O. Box 1832, Evanston, IL 60204), 1983. ($11.95).

Circles of Friends. R. Perske. Nashville: Abingdon Press, 1988.

Developmental Disabilities: A Life Span Approach. J.L. Matson & A. Marchetti (Eds.) Philadelphia: Grune & Stratton, 1988. ($45.00).

Family, Government and Long-Term Care: The Case for People with Mental Retardation. Plymouth Meeting, PA: Ken-Crest Centers (One Plymouth Meeting, S-620, Plymouth Meeting, PA 19462), 1989.

Friendships and Community Connections between People with and without Developmental Disabilities. A. Novak Amado. Baltimore: Paul H. Brookes, 1993.

It's Never Too Early - It's Never Too Late: A Booklet about Personal Futures Planning. B. Mount & K. Zwernik. Minnesota's Bookstore (117 University Ave., St. Paul, MN 55155, (612) 297-3000), 1988. ($5.95).

Lifeplan: A Workbook for Assisting Parents of People with Developmental Disabilities in Thinking about the Future. W.T. Allen. Rohnert Park, CA: California Institute on Human Services (Sonoma State University, 1801 E. Cotati Ave., Rohnert Park, CA 94928), 1989. ($26.50).

Planning for the Disabled Child. A.H. Wernz. Milwaukee: Northwestern Mutual Life Insurance Co., 1984.

Planning for the Future: Providing a Meaningful Life for a Child with a Disability after Your Death. L.M. Russell, S.M. Joseph, A. Grant, & R. Fee. Evanston, IL: American Publishing Co., 1993.

APPENDIX C

RESOURCES FOR ADVOCACY

The organizations below can provide information about disability issues in general, as well as about advocating for the rights of individuals with disabilities. Many distribute newsletters, fact sheets, and other publications. Call and request a publications list.

The Arc (a national organization on mental retardation)
500 E. Border St., Suite 300
P.O. Box 1047
Arlington, TX 76010
(817) 261-6003; (800) 433-5255
(817) 277-0553 (TDD)
(817) 277-3491 (FAX)

Association for the Care of Children's Health
7910 Woodmont Ave.
Suite 300
Bethesda, MD, 20814
(301) 654-6549; (301) 986-4553 (FAX)

Autism Network International (ANI)
P.O. Box 1545
Lawrence, KS 66044

Autism Society of America
7910 Woodmont Ave., Suite 650
Bethesda, MD 20814
(800) 3AU-TISM; (301) 657-0881
(301) 657-0869 (FAX)

Canadian Association for Community Living
Kinsmen Building
York University
4700 Keele St.
North York, ON
Canada M3J 1P3
(416) 661-9611; (416) 661-5701 (FAX)

Center for Accessible Housing
North Carolina State University
School of Design
Box 8613
Raleigh, NC 27695-8613
(919) 515-3082; (919) 515-3023 (FAX)

Children's Defense Fund
25 E Street NW
Washington, DC 20001
(202) 628-8787; (202) 662-3520 (FAX)

Christian Council on Persons with Disabilities
1324 Yosemite Blvd.
Modesto, CA 95354
(209) 524-7993

Council for Exceptional Children
1920 Association Drive
Reston, VA 22091-1589
(703) 620-3660; (703) 264-9494 (FAX)

DREDF (Disability Rights Education and Defense Fund)
2212 Sixth St.
Berkeley, CA 94710
(510) 644-2555

Keshet-Jewish Parents of Children with Special Needs
3525 W. Peterson, Suite T-17
Chicago, IL 60659
(312) 588-0551

National Association of Protection and Advocacy Systems
900 Second Street NE, Suite 221
Washington, DC 20002
(202) 408-9514; (202) 408-9520 (FAX)

National Catholic Office for Persons with Disabilities
P.O. Box 29113
Washington, DC 20017
(202) 529-2933 (Voice/TDD); (202) 529-4678

National Down Syndrome Congress
1605 Chantilly Dr., Suite 250
Atlanta, GA 30324
(800) 232-6372; (404) 633-1555
(404) 633-2817 (FAX)

National Mental Health Association
1021 Prince St.
Alexandria, VA 22314-2971
(800) 969-6642; (703) 684-7722
(703) 684-5968 (FAX)

NICHCY (National Information Center for Children and Youth with Disabilities)
P.O. Box 1492
Washington, DC 20013
(800) 695-0285; (202) 884-8200

National Information System and Clearinghouse Center for Developmental Disabilities
University of South Carolina
Benson Building
Columbia, SC 29208
(800) 922-9234; (800) 922-1107 (in SC)
(803) 777-6058 (FAX)

National Organization on Disability
910 16th Street NW, Suite 600
Washington, DC 20006
(202) 293-5960; (202) 229-1187 (in MD)
(800) 248-ABLE

National Parent Network on Disabilities
1600 Prince Street
Suite 115
Alexandria, VA 22314
(703) 684-NPND; (703) 684-6763 (Voice/TDD)

Pacer Center (Parent Advocacy Coalition for Educational Rights)
4826 Chicago Ave. South
Minneapolis, MN 55417
(612) 827-2966

United Cerebral Palsy Associations
1660 L St., NW, Suite 700
Washington, DC 20036
(800) 872-5827; (202) 776-0406

INDICATIONS
OF ABUSE

There are several types of abuse. Physical abuse may include slapping, pinching, or shoving. Sexual abuse is the term used to describe any unwanted sexual contact, and psychological abuse refers to ridicule, humiliation, screaming, shouting, etc. Other types of mistreatment can include neglecting someone's needs or violating his civil rights.

The next few pages list several indicators of different types of abuse as identified by James Lauer, Ira Laurie, Marsha Salur, and Diane Broadhurt in their publication *The Role of the Mental Health Professional in the Prevention and Treatment of Child Abuse and Neglect.* The writers of the manual caution, however, that these signs are most likely indicative of abuse if they are part of a pattern rather than a one-time occurrence. You can use the list to help decide whether to begin investigating the possibility of abuse and/or to terminate a relationship. Please keep in mind that these guidelines were written for administrators of residential programs for dealing with their staff. The terminology may be a little awkward from a parent's perspective, but the concepts should be helpful.

Physical Abuse

Physical Signs

1. Unexplained bruises or welts
- on several different areas
- in various stages of healing (bruises of different colors, old and new scars)
- in the shape of instrument used to inflict them
- spiral fractures
- shaken child syndrome

2. Unexplained burns
- in the shape of instrument used to inflict them (cigarettes, rope, iron)
- caused by immersion into hot liquid (may be glove-like or sock-like)

3. Unexplained lacerations or abrasions
- to mouth, lips, gums
- to external genitals
- on the backs of arms, legs, torso

4. Unexplained skeletal injuries
- fractures of skull or face
- multiple fractures
- stiff, swollen joints
- bald spots from hair pulling
- missing or loosened teeth
- human-size bite marks, especially if adult size and recurrent
- detached retina (from shaking or hitting)
- clothing inappropriate for the weather (concealing injuries)
- emaciated
- distended stomach

5. Consistent hunger/malnutrition

6. **Poor hygiene**
   - lice
   - body odor
7. **Lacks appropriate/necessary clothing**
8. **Unattended physical problems or medical needs**
   - lack of proper immunization
   - gross dental problems
   - needs glasses, hearing aids
9. **Constant lack of supervision**
   - especially in dangerous situations or circumstances
10. **Constant fatigue/listlessness**

Client's (your child's) Behavior
1. **Developmental lags**
   - physical, emotional, intellectual
2. **Seeks attention/affection**
   - hypochondria

Emotional Maltreatment

Physical Signs
1. **Health problems**
   - obesity
   - skin disorders (acne)
   - speech disorders (stuttering)
   - asthma, allergies, ulcers
2. **Infantile behavior**
3. **Pants/bedwetting**
4. **Thumbsucking**
5. **Failure-to-thrive in infancy**
6. **Poor Appetite**
7. **Sleep disorders**
8. **Other indicators listed with physical abuse**

Client's (your child's) Behavior
1. **Fear of caregivers or parents**
2. **Injuries inflicted by caregivers or parents**

3. Unbelievable reasons for injuries
4. Extremes in behavior
- very aggressive
- very withdrawn
- submissive, overly compliant, caters to adults
- hyperactive
- depressed/apathetic

5. Easily frightened/fearful
- of others: caregivers, adults, etc.
- of physical contact
- of going home

6. Destructive to self/others
- poor social relations
- craves affection
- indiscriminate attachment to strangers
- relates poorly to peers
- manipulates adults to get attention

7. Demonstrates poor self-concept
- suicidal

Sexual Abuse

Physical Signs
1. Difficulty walking
2. Torn, stained, or bloody underclothing
3. Abnormalities in genital/anal areas
- itching, pain, swelling
- bruises, bleeding
- frequent urinary or yeast infections
- pain on urination
- vaginal/penal discharge
- poor sphincter control

4. Venereal disease
5. Pregnancy
6. Psychosomatic illness
7. Client's Behavior
8. States that he/she has been abused

9. Sexual knowledge beyond age

 displays bizarre, sophisticated sexual behavior

10. Regression to earlier developmental stage

11. Other indicators listed with physical abuse

BIBLIOGRAPHY

Amado, A., Conklin F. and Wells, J. *Friends: A Manual for Connecting Persons with Disabilities and Community Members*. St. Paul, MN: Human Services Research and Development Center, 1990.

Association for Retarded Citizens of the United States. *How to Provide for Their Future: Suggestions for Parents Concerned with Providing Lifetime Support for a Child with a Developmental Disability*. Arlington, TX: The Arc, 1989.

Bavolek, S. and Mattei, A. *People Do Matter . . . There Is No Excuse for Abuse: A Curriculum Developed to Assist All Staff in Preventing Abuse*. Albany: New York State Office of Mental Retardation and Developmental Disabilities, 1987.

Berkobien, R. *A Family Handbook on Future Planning*. Arlington, TX: The Arc, 1991.

Bersani, H. *Assuring Residential Quality: Issues, Approaches and Instruments*. Syracuse, NY: Syracuse University, 1989.

Bradley, V. and Bersani, H. *Quality Assurance for Individuals with Developmental Disabilities: It's Everybody's Business*. Baltimore: Paul H. Brookes Publishing Co., 1990.

Center on Human Policy. *The Community Imperative: A Refutation of All Arguments in Support of Institutionalizing Anybody Because of Mental Retardation*. Syracuse, NY: Syracuse University, 1979.

Chadsey-Rusch, J., DeStefano, L., O'Reilly, M., Gonzalez, P., Collet-Klingenberg, L. "Assessing the Loneliness of Workers with Mental Retardation," *Mental Retardation* 30, No. 2 (1992) 85-92.

Conroy, J.W. and Bradley, V.J. *The Pennhurst Longitudinal Study: A Report of Five Years of Research and Analysis.* Philadelphia: Temple University Developmental Disabilities Center. Boston: Human Services Research Institute, 1985.

Faber, A. and Mazlish, E. *How to Talk So Kids Will Listen and Listen So Kids Will Talk.* New York: Avon Books, 1982.

Gardner, Howard. *Frames of Mind: The Theory of Multiple Intelligences.* New York: BasicBooks, A Division of HarperCollins Publishers, 1993.

Hill, B.K., Rotegard, L.R., and Bruiniks, R.H. "Quality of Life of Mentally Retarded People in Residential Care," *Social Work* 29; No. 3 (1984) 275-281.

Hahn, H. and Stout, R. *The Internet Yellow Pages.* Second Edition. Berkeley: Osbourne McGraw-Hill, 1995.

Janicki, M. *Building the Future: Planning and Community Development in Aging and Developmental Disabilities.* Albany: New York State Office of Mental Retardation and Developmental Disabilities, 1991.

Janicki, M. and Keefe, R. *Integration Experiences Casebook: Program Ideas in Aging and Developmental Disabilities.* Albany: New York State Office of Mental Retardation and Developmental Disabilities, 1992.

Kaufman, A., Adams, J., Campbell, V. "Permanency Planning by Older Parents Who Care for Adult Children with Mental Retardation," *Mental Retardation* 29, No. 5 (1991) 293-300.

Kobe, F., Rojahn, J., and Schroeder, S. "Predictors of Urgency of Out-of-Home Placement Needs," *Mental Retardation* 29, No. 6 (1991) 323-328.

Kubler-Ross, E. *On Death and Dying.* New York: MacMillan Publishing Company, 1969.

Kugel, R. and Wolfensberger, W. (Eds.) *Changing Patterns in Residential Services for the Mentally Retarded.* Washington, D.C.: President's Committee on Mental Retardation, 1969.

Legislative Budget and Finance Committee, A Joint Committee of the Pennsylvania General Assembly. *Report on Salary Levels and Their Impact on Quality of Care for Client Contact Workers in Community-based MH/MR and Child Day Care Programs.* Harrisburg, PA, 1989.

LePore, P. and Janicki, M. *The Wit to Win: How to Integrate Older Persons with Developmental Disabilities into Community Aging Programs.* Albany: New York State Office for the Aging, 1991.

Moore, C. *A Reader's Guide for Parents of Children with Mental, Physical, or Emotional Disabilities.* Bethesda, MD: Woodbine House, 1990.

Mount, B. *Imperfect Change: Easing the Tensions of Person-Centered Work.* Manchester, CT: Communitas, Inc., 1990.

Mount, B. and Zwernik, K. *It's Never Too Early, It's Never Too Late: A Booklet about Personal Futures Planning.* St. Paul, MN: Metropolitan Council, 1988.

New Hats, Inc. *Using Natural Supports in Community Integration.* Salt Lake City, Utah, 1990.

O'Connell, M. *The Gift of Hospitality: Opening the Doors of Community Life to People with Disabilities*. Chicago: Northwestern University, 1988.

O'Connell, M. *Getting Connected: How to Find Out about Groups and Organizations in Your Neighborhood*. Chicago: Northwestern University, 1988.

Pennsylvania Department of Public Welfare. *Everyday Lives*. Harrisburg, PA: Pennsylvania Department of Public Welfare, Office of Mental Retardation, 1991.

Rader, H. and Simpson, J. "Effective Parent Advocacy: How to Take Charge." *Exceptional Parent*, September, 1993.

Scheerenberger, R. *A History of Mental Retardation: A Quarter Century of Promise*. Baltimore: Paul H. Brookes Publishing Co., 1987.

INDEX

Abuse, 7-8, 36-37, 118-20, 199-203
Acceptance, 172-73
Accessibility, 60-61, 97, 99
Activities, 22, 30-31, 35-36, 50,
    154-55
  of daily living, 148, 153
  to expand network, 52-67
  extracurricular, 78
Adaptations, 36, 72, 171
Administrators, 75, 118
Advisory councils, 54
Advocacy, 16, 21, 27, 33, 42, 65-66,
    164, 168, 178-88
  groups, 3, 39, 64, 75, 82, 163,
    195-98
  in the schools, 72
Aerobics, 58
Agencies, 1-2, 55, 146, 148, 150, 153,
    156, 158, 170
Age of majority, 148, 165
Aides, 73, 74, 75, 80
Airports, 58

Alcohol abuse, 58
Alternative health, 58
American Civil Liberties Union, 180
American Journal of Mental
    Retardation, 172
American Red Cross, 58
Americans with Disabilities Act (ADA),
    70, 98, 180, 181, 187, 190
America Online, 187
Anger, 172
Appliance use, 24
Applications, 26
Approval, 43
Aptitude, 42-43, 45-50, 51, 55, 71,
    148, 154
Arcade, 57
Art, 57
Assistive devices, 38-39, 50, 72, 80
Association for Retarded Citizens
    (The Arc), 59, 162, 164, 187
Attitudes, 34-40, 98, 174
Autonomy, 3, 37

Background, 65
Banking, 25, 58
Bargaining, 172
Baseball, 79
Bathing, 8, 24, 35, 149, 152-53
Bed making, 24
Behavior, 61, 99
    modification, 8-9, 73, 80
    problems, 13, 150, 151
Benefits, 25, 26, 161
Bicycle shops, 58
Big Brothers, 59, 64
Big Sisters, 59, 64
Birth control, 25
Black, Thom, 47
Board and supervision facility, 153
Boarding homes, 152
Board of Education of the Borough of
    Clementon School District v.
    Oberti, 76
Books, 59, 80
"Boomerangers," 168
Boredom, 45
Born to Fly: How to Discover and
    Encourage Your Child's Natural
    Talent, 47
Bosses, 26
Braille typewriters, 80
Budgeting, 25
Business, 4, 26, 55
Bus use, 25, 58, 103
Cab use, 25, 58
California, 184
Camp counselors, 41
Camping, 57, 70, 150
Caregivers, 2, 14, 33, 36, 118
Cars, 58
Center for Evaluation, Development
    and Research, 79
Center for Urban Affairs and Policy
    Research, 52
Chicago Institute on Disability and
    Human Development, 6

Child care agencies, 59
Choice, 3, 4, 21, 37, 38, 148, 151
Church, 36, 53, 54, 55, 59, 82, 104-
    105, 153, 156
Citizen advisory committees, 54
Citizenship, 3
Civil defense office, 55
Civil Rights Office, 76
Classes, 59
Cleaning, 24
Clothing care, 24, 34-35, 38
Clustered apartment programs,
    151-52
Coaches, 41, 49, 78
Coffee shops, 58
Cognitive development, 43, 59
Cognitive disabilities, 5-6, 51-52
    needs of people with, 3, 23, 70
    skills of people with, 43-45, 46-47,
    49-50
Colorado, 72-73
Colorado Springs, 72-73
"Common Assets of Mentally
    Retarded People That Are
    Commonly Not Acknowledged,"
    43-45
Communication, 38, 39, 50, 80, 87,
    100, 103-105, 182-83. See also
    Speech; Language
Community, 54, 58, 70, 98, 130, 156,
    174-75
    building, 2-3, 147
    center, 36, 53, 56, 57, 58, 70
    college, 59, 63, 98
    experiences, 4, 13-14, 25, 48, 51-52
    organizations, 53
    readiness, 49-50
    services, 6, 151
Community Life Project, The, 52, 53
Comprehension, 50
CompuServe, 187
Computers, 39, 80
Concerts, 57

Confidence, 38
Congregate housing, 6
Consistency, 3, 15-16
Control, 3, 7, 27, 38, 148, 151.
    See also Choice
Convenience stores, 58
"Conversation Start Up Kit," 103-105
Cooking, 24, 152-53
Cooperative Master Trust, 161-62
Council for Developmentally
    Disabled & Handicapped
    Persons, 59
Counseling, 92
Counselor, 58
County commissioner, 54
County secretary, 54
Coworkers, 26, 27, 66
Creativity, 45
Crime, 13-14
Crossing the River: Creating a
    Conceptual Revolution in
    Community and Disability, 7
CTB/McGraw Hill, 49
Curriculum, 36, 72, 80
Dancing, 43, 59
Dates, 59
Day programs, 65, 150
Decor, 35
Denial, 172
Dental care, 24, 34-35, 58
Department of Developmental
    Disabilities, 146
Department of Education, 39, 76, 148
Department of Housing and Urban
    Development (HUD), 157
Department of Labor, 38
Department of Mental Retardation, 146
Department of Rehabilitation, 39
Dependency, 21, 23
Depression, 172
Diagnosis, 146
Diet, 24
"Dignity of Risk, The," 121

Direct care staff, 11. *See also* Staffing
Directness, 44
Directories, 52-53
Discretionary Trust, 161
Dishwashing, 24
District of Columbia, 6
Documentation, 181
Down syndrome, 32-33
Dressing, 24, 34-35, 90, 152-53
Driving, 25
Drug abuse, 58
Due process, 75, 76, 180
Dues, 61
Dusting, 24
Eating, 24
Education, 38, 59, 70-82, 104-105, 152
Educators, 42, 49, 72, 75, 77, 80
Elbern Publications, 49
Eligibility, 146, 151
Emergencies, 25
Empathy, 43, 46, 106
Employers, 26
Employment, 26, 34-35, 58, 64,
    66, 149
Empowerment, 37-40
Encouragement, 43, 51
Encyclopedia of Associations, 53
Enjoyment, 44
Environmental groups, 53
Environmental Issues Checklist, 60-61
Estates, 159-61, 175
Everyday Lives, 2-3, 4
Expectations, 86-88
Exploration, 23
Eye-gaze controls, 38
Faber, Adele, 87
Facilitators, 65
Fair Market Value, 157
"Family Handbook on Future
    Planning, A," 164-65
Family living, 150
Fathers of Children with Disabilities,
    187

Fear, 51, 87, 110
Finances, 25, 44, 51, 58, 145-47, 152, 159-63
Fire safety, 25
Fire station, 58
Flexibility, 7, 17, 51, 178
FM systems, 80
Focus, 44-45
Following directions, 24
Food stamps, 58
Foreclosures, 158
Foster care, 6, 150
Fourth National Study of Public Spending for Mental Retardation and Developmental Disabilities in the United States, 6
Freedom, 3
Friends, 21, 23, 25, 27-28, 36
    developing, 41, 42, 59-60, 64, 73, 82, 102-105
    through key persons, 96-99
    through groups, 99-100, 116-18
    maintaining, 105-109, 148
    roles of, 65, 85, 135
Funding, 147, 148, 151, 152, 153, 154, 155-56, 178
Gardner, Howard, 45, 46, 48, 51
Geist Picture Interest Inventory, Revised, 49
Generosity, 43
Gentleness, 44
Georgia, 186
"Getting Connected: How to Find Out about Groups and Organizations in Your Neighborhood," 52
"Gift of Hospitality, The: Opening the Doors of Community Life to People with Disabilities," 52
Gifts, 42-43, 45-50, 51, 55, 71, 148, 154
Goals, 38, 65, 70, 73
Goethe, 32
Government, 54, 146, 170, 184-85

benefits, 25, 26, 161
    funding, 147, 148, 151, 153, 155
    guidelines, 4, 13, 65, 75, 150, 159, 178
    offices, 1-2, 58, 146
Governor's Committee on Employment for the Handicapped, 59
Graffam, Joseph, 172
Grants, federal, 76
Grief, 172-73
Groceries, 24, 58, 104
Grooming, 8, 24, 34-35, 58
Group homes, 6, 7, 70, 151, 153
Groups, 55. See also Agencies; Advocacy; groups
    joining, 52-55, 64, 99-100
    forming, 55-57, 101
Guardianship, 162-66, 171, 175
Hairstyling, 24, 34-35
Handicap BBS Lists, 187
Hobbies, 22, 25, 42, 47, 59
Holland v. Sacramento City Unified School District, 76
"Holy innocents," 30, 45
Honesty, 44
Hospice, 59
Hospitals, 53, 58
Hotels, 53, 58
Housekeeping, 24, 151
Housing, 147, 157-58. See also individual types of housing
Housing cooperatives, 158
Housing Finance Agencies (HFA), 158
Housing vouchers, 157-58
How To Talk So Kids Will Listen and Listen So Kids Will Talk, 87
Humanistic model, 6, 9
Human Relations Commission, 181
Human Rights Commission, 76
Human service, 58, 146, 151
    field, 5, 49, 154
    system, 2, 9, 11, 17, 62, 65, 85, 156
    dependency on, 21, 23

workers, 31, 41-42, 47, 48. *See also* Staffing
Inclusion, 70-82
Independence, 4, 148, 150, 153, 168
Indiana, 79
Individuality, 3, 6, 22, 37, 73
Individualized Education Program (IEP), 38, 42, 73, 75, 80, 115
Individualized Habilitation Plans (IHP), 65, 115
Individuals with Disabilities Education Act (IDEA), 75-76, 180, 190
In Praise of Parents, 179
Institutional services, 5-6, 32-33, 153-54
Insurance, 160-61, 180-81
Intellectual development, 43, 45-47, 48
Intelligence Quotient (IQ), 46
Intentional communities, 156
Interests, 42, 47, 48, 49, 51-54, 59-61, 63, 78
Internet, 187
Internet Yellow Pages, 187
Interpersonal skills, 46
Interviewing, 26
Intrapersonal skills, 46
Ironing, 24
Isolation, 8, 51, 62, 105, 130-31, 151, 164, 171, 172
Jerry Lewis telethon, 30
Joint property ownership, 162
Kinesthetics, 46
Kubler-Ross, Elisabeth, 172
Labeling, 46, 73
Labor. *See* Staffing
Language, 38, 45, 46
Lanterman Act, 184
Laundry, 24, 58
Lawn care, 24
Lawyers, 59
Leadership, 46
Least Restrictive Environment (LRE), 71, 76

Legislative Coalition, 59
Leisure, 22, 25, 38, 54, 57
Libraries, 53, 55, 58, 104
Limitations, 29, 42, 47
Little League, 79
Location, 21, 22, 31, 35-36
Logic, 46
Long-term care, 5, 29, 32. *See also* Institutional services; Residential programs
Los Angeles, 49
Love, 43, 44
Lutheran Social Services, 9
Magazines, 53, 59
Mainstreaming, 70-82
Malls, 58
"Matchmakers," 64
Materialism, 44
Math, 46
Mazlish, Elaine, 87
McKnight, John, 2-3
Meals, 24, 148, 153
Meals on Wheels, 58
Medicaid, 58, 161
Medical care, 24, 25, 58, 79, 149, 151, 153, 154
Medical model, 6
Medicare, 58
Medication, 7-8, 24
Meetings, 42-43, 60
Mental retardation. *See* Cognitive disabilities
Mental Retardation Association, 59
Mentoring, 66, 186
Money management, 8, 25
Mopping, 24
Motels, 58
"Mothers From Hell," 184
Motivation, 46
Motorcycles, 58
Mount, Beth, 65
Movement, 46
Movies, 57

Multiple intelligences, 45-46, 48
Museums, 57
Music, 46, 48, 59, 78
National Association of State Boards of Education (NASBE), 72
Needs, 3-4, 65-66, 154
  individual, 20, 23, 92-93, 147
Negative images, 29-33, 34-40
Neglect, 7-8
Neighborhoods, 53, 54, 59, 66, 72, 76, 154, 156
Networking, 26, 39, 51, 61-66, 70, 82-83, 129-31, 156, 167
  with siblings, 85, 87
Nevada, 6, 154
New Hampshire, 6
New Hats, Inc., 55-56, 103, 106
New Jersey, 6, 154, 184
Newspapers, 52-53, 59
New York, 6, 118
Non-Reading Aptitude Battery, 49
Non-verbal, 50, 102
Northwestern University, 52
Nursing homes, 153, 154-55
Oberti v. Board of Education of the Borough of Clementon School District, 76
O'Brien, John, 186
Occupational therapy, 58
O'Connell, Mary, 52, 53, 55, 61, 66
Office of Compliance, 76
Office of Developmental Disabilities, 146
Office of Human Services, 65
Office of Mental Retardation, 2, 118, 146
Organizations. See Agencies; Advocacy; groups
Parent Advocacy, 120
Parental role, 4, 78
Parent Education and Assistance for Kids (PEAK), 72-73, 76
Parent Education Network (PEN), 179, 180, 182

Parent education training centers, 76
Parent funded alternatives, 155-56
Parent Panthers, 187
Parks, 53, 57
Parties, 59, 82
Passion, 3
Patience, 44
Pennsylvania, 98
Pennsylvania Coalition for Citizens with Disabilities, 179
Pennsylvania Legislative and Budget Finance Committee, 12
Pennsylvania Office of Mental Retardation, 2
"People Do Matter: There Is No Excuse for Abuse," 118
People First of Washington, 3
Perception, 29-33, 34-35
Permanency, 3, 15-16, 17
Personal care, 8, 24, 34-35, 58
Personal care facility, 152-53
Personal Futures Planning, 65
Personal information, knowledge of, 25
Personality, 43-45, 48, 50
Person Centered Planning, 64-66
Photo boards, 38-39
Physical therapy, 58
Placement, 1-2, 148
Planned Parenthood, 59
Planning, 64-66, 178
  future, 14-16, 27-28, 51, 69
  needs assessment, 21-27
Plays, 57
"Poison darts," 36-37
Police, 25, 55, 58, 59
Political parties, 53
Popovich, Elaine, 9
Possessions, 35, 44, 58
Post office, 58
Preferences, 21, 50, 65
Principals, 75, 81
Privacy, 3

Problems Making Friends checklist, 112-13
Problem solving, 21, 25, 46, 55, 57
Procedures, 4, 13
Professional associations, 59
Professionals, 41, 42-43, 48
Prosperity, 3
Protection and Advocacy office, 188
Protective order, 164
Protégé, 186
Psychologist, 49, 115
Psychotropic drugs, 7-8
Pull-out programs, 73
Punctuality, 26
Quality of life, 11
Radio, 59
Reading Free Vocational Interest Inventory, Revised, 49
Reciprocity, 42
Recognition, 3
Recreation, 25, 38, 54, 57
    programs, 7, 52-53, 70, 78
Recruitment, 8, 13
Rehabilitation Act of 1973, 76, 190
Relationships, 3, 25, 29, 36, 59, 65
    abusive, 118-20
    developing, 41, 42, 43-45, 46-47, 51, 59-60, 62, 64, 73, 82
    expanding, 52-60, 66, 102-105, 116-18
    maintaining, 105-109
    siblings, 49, 85-94
    troubleshooting, 111-17, 135-37
Relatives, 27, 49, 51, 59, 62, 148, 149, 183-84
Reliability, 3, 15-16, 17
Religion, 45, 54, 59, 82
Removing Obstacles Checklist, 114-15
Rental certificates, 157
Repairs, 24
Representative payee, 162
Research Bulletin, 79

Residential programs, 4-7, 22, 26, 31, 38, 145-56, 175. *See also individual types of housing*
    socialization and, 58, 62, 65, 66
Respect, 5
Respite care, 56, 59, 149, 150
Responsibility, 4, 79, 87, 135, 137-41
Restaurants, 58, 104
Retention, 8, 13
Rhode Island, 6
Rights, 59, 75, 154, 180
Roles, 65
Rules, 4, 13
Sacramento City Unified School District v. Holland, 76
Safety, 13-14, 25, 168
Salt Lake City, 55
School, 38, 59, 70-82, 104-105, 152
Schwartz, David, 7, 8
Scouting, 79
Seating, 80
Section 504, 76
Section 8 housing, 157-58
Security, 3
Segregated programs, 71, 74-78, 81
Self-esteem, 79
Self-fulfilling prophecy, 31-32
Semi-independent living, 152
Service models, 9, 11. *See also* Humanistic model; Human service, system; Medical model
Sex, 25, 147
Sher, Barbara, 46-47
Shopping, 24, 57, 151, 153
Siblings, 49, 85-94
Skills, 42-43, 45-50, 51, 55, 71, 148, 154
Small group housing, 6
Social and Prevocational Information Battery (SPIB), 49
Social convention, 43

Socialization, 39-40, 43, 52-57, 59, 154, 174. *See also* Groups; Leisure; Relationships
appropriate, 25, 50, 80, 104-105, 107-109
frequency of, 21, 67
variety of, 5, 27-28, 82-83, 113
Social Security, 58, 152, 161, 162
Spas, 58
Spatial reasoning, 46, 48
Special Olympics, 35, 36
Speech, 38, 39, 50
Speech-language pathologist, 39, 49, 115
Speech synthesizers, 80
Spirituality, 45, 54, 59
Spontaneity, 43
Sports, 52, 57, 78, 104-105
Staffing, 6-7, 8, 11-13, 41-42, 62, 67, 147, 151, 153, 156
State representative, 54
Stereotypes, 29-33, 35, 45, 174
Stress, 11, 173
Suctioning, 80
Supplemental Security Income (SSI), 152, 159, 161
Supplemental Trust, 161
Support, 21, 23, 33, 36, 65, 145, 167-69, 183-88
classroom, 72, 75, 76, 77
checklist, 24-28, 134
needed for community living, 41, 51, 52, 71, 133-35, 152, 154
in home, 149-50
Supported living, 149
Sweeping, 24
Swimming, 57
Synagogues, 55
Syracuse University, 29
Talents, 42-43, 45-50, 51, 55, 71, 148, 154
Talking communication device, 38, 39
Taxes, 25

Teachers, 42, 49, 72, 75, 77, 80
Telephone, 53, 148
Television, 59
Testing, 46, 49, 79
Theater, 57
Therapy, 30-31, 38, 58, 63
Thrift shops, 58
Ticket purchases, 25
Timeliness, 26
Timing, 35-36
Toileting, 8, 24
Token concepts, 42
Tolerance, 44
Toothbrushing, 24
Totten Trust, 160
Township, 54
"Toxic Talk," 36-37
Toys, 39
Training, 150, 152-53, 179
Train use, 25, 58
Transportation, 25, 57, 62, 67, 147, 169
Travel, 25, 57, 58
Trust, 44
Trust funds, 159, 160-62
Turner, Jim, 172
Turnover, staff, 11-12
United Cerebral Palsy, 187
United States Department of Labor, 49
United States Employment Service, 49
United Way, 53
University of Illinois, 6
"Using Natural Supports in Community Integration," 56-57, 103
US News and World Report, 184
Utah, 55
Vacuuming, 24
Vehicle maintenance, 25
Vermont, 6
Visual impairment, 80
Vocational rehabilitation office, 58
Vocational Rehabilitation Services, 59
Voice-input computers, 39
Volunteers, 53, 55, 58, 59

Vulnerability, 26-27, 107-109, 154
Washington Township, 54
Weight training, 58
Western Psychological Services, 49
Wills, 69, 159, 163, 166, 175
Winning Ways, 72
Wishcraft, 46-47
Wolfensberger, Wolf, 29, 30, 31, 32, 34
    on skills of the disabled, 43, 44,
        45, 48
Work, 26, 34-35, 50, 58, 63, 64, 66,
    70, 149, 153
Workshops, 7, 70
Wright, H. Norman, 36
YMCA, 36, 57
Yoga, 58
"You and I," 9, 10
YWCA, 57
Zoo, 57

About the Author:

Linda J. Stengle has worked for more than fifteen years with people with disabilities and their families. She was formerly the Executive Director of two Arcs in Pennsylvania and a private provider of services for people with mental retardation, and has also worked as a professional advocate, vocational services director, and residential manager. Currently, Stengle is a freelance writer and consultant, working with advocacy organizations in Pennsylvania to address the issue of waiting lists for services. She was the principal author of **Repatriation: The Key to Community**, published by The Arc of Pennsylvania in Harrisburg. The parent of two, Stengle lives with her family in Boyertown, Pennsylvania.